THE

WEIRDLE

GAME BOOK

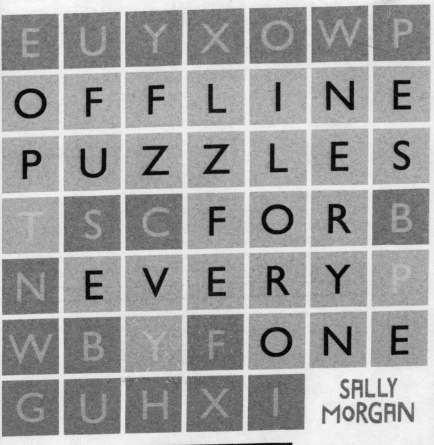

OFFLINE

PUZZLES

FOR

EVERY

ONE

SALLY MORGAN

■ SCHOLASTIC

Published in the UK by Scholastic, 2022
1 London Bridge, London, SE1 9BA
Scholastic Ireland, 89E Lagan Road, Dublin Industrial Estate, Glasnevin,
Dublin, D11 HP5F

Written by Sally Morgan © Scholastic, 2022

ISBN 978 07023 2377 5

A CIP catalogue record for this book is available from the British Library.

Printed by CPI Group (UK) Ltd, Croydon CR0 4YY
Paper made from wood grown in sustainable forests and other
controlled sources.

1 3 5 7 9 10 8 6 4 2

www.scholastic.co.uk

CONTENTS

WELCOME TO WEIRDLE:

A WONDERFULLY WORDY GAME BOOK!

- -

In this book you will find word searches, riddles, crosswords, hink pinks, cryptograms, kangaroo words, word ladders, anagrams and many other brain-busting word games that you can complete offline and IRL (In Real Life).

Some of these puzzles may be familiar to you, whereas others are unlike anything you have ever seen before, but like all word puzzles they can:

- banish boredom
- increase your vocabulary
- sharpen your spelling skills
- improve your memory
- soothe stress
- and befuddle your family.

You might find some of these puzzles a bit tricky, but never fear, if any of the word games inside this book prove to be more frustrating than fun, turn to page 255 onwards to find the solution.

So what are you waiting for? Grab a pen and see how many weirdly wonderful WIFI-free word games you can conquer.

Who knows, you may even learn a new weird word or two!

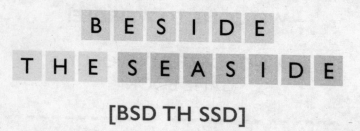

[BSD TH SSD]

Find the missing vowels to complete the perfect day at the beach.

Which one would you be unlucky to see at a British beach?

A E I O U

Example:

SNDCSTL

S A N D C A S T L E

1. STCKFRCK

☐☐☐☐☐ ☐☐
☐☐☐☐

2. BCH

☐☐☐☐☐

3. PNCHNDJDY

☐☐☐☐☐ ☐☐☐
☐☐☐☐

4. FRGRNDRDS

☐☐☐☐☐☐☐☐☐☐
☐☐☐☐☐

5. CCRM

☐☐☐ ☐☐☐☐☐

6. CLLLY

☐☐☐ ☐☐☐☐☐

7. PBBL

☐☐☐☐☐☐

8. RCKPL

☐☐☐☐☐☐☐☐

9. BCHHT

☐☐☐☐☐ ☐☐☐

10. SVNR

□□□□□□□□

11. SSHLL

□□□□□□□□

12. OCN

□□□□□

13. WV

□□□□

14. BCKTNDSPD

□□□□□□□□□□

15. GRTWHTSHRK

16. SNSHN

17. STRFSH

18. SNCRM

19. TWL

Answers on page 255.

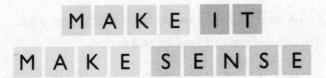

MAKE IT MAKE SENSE

---

ach of the following statements contains one word that makes it incorrect. Can you replace one word in each of sentences to make it make sense?

Example:

Billie Eilish had a hit in 2016 with the song Arctic Eyes.

Billie Eilish had a hit in 2016 with the song ~~Arctic~~ Eyes.

Billie Eilish had a hit in 2016 with the song <u>OCEAN</u> Eyes.

1. Sir Isaac Newton was a famous scientist who discovered laws of gravity and lotion.

☐ ☐ ☐ ☐ ☐ ☐

2. The Apprentice is a television program on the BBC presented by Lord Alan Sweetener.

☐ ☐ ☐ ☐ ☐

3. The Great Fire of Loughborough took place in the year 1666.

☐ ☐ ☐ ☐ ☐ ☐

4. Actress Rosalie Chiang provided the voice of character Mei Lee in the 2022 Pixar film 'Being Red'

☐ ☐ ☐ ☐ ☐ ☐ ☐

5. Michael Omari is the real name of British slime and hiphop artist Stormzy.

☐ ☐ ☐ ☐ ☐

6. The fifth wife of King Henry VIII was named Katherine Jenkins.

☐ ☐ ☐ ☐ ☐ ☐

7. Melanie C, Pixie Lott and will.i.am were all performance judges on UK baking competition The Voice Kids.

☐ ☐ ☐ ☐ ☐ ☐ ☐

8. John Lennon, Paul McCartney, George Harrison and Ringo Moon were all members of a band named The Beatles.

☐ ☐ ☐ ☐ ☐

9. US recording artist Beyoncé biggest hit of 2008 was her track, "Single Bells (Put a Ring on It)"

☐ ☐ ☐ ☐ ☐ ☐

10. Sir Ian McKellen travelled to New Zealand to make 'The Lord of the Flies' trilogy of films.

☐ ☐ ☐ ☐ ☐

Answers on page 255.

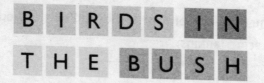

BIRDS IN THE BUSH

See if you can find the birds hidden amongst these wordy weeds.

1. Their calls grow loud at dusk.

2. We found a nest in the roof in Chester Cathedral.

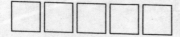

3. Quite the heartthrob in the winter.

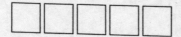

4. A proud hunter but a touch awkward.

5. What's to crave now the Tower has them?

☐☐☐☐☐☐☐☐☐☐

6. Thinking fish err on the side of caution.

☐☐☐☐☐☐☐☐☐☐

7. The tallest, and most rich of its feathery friends.

☐☐☐☐☐☐☐

8. Sneaky thieves of the shore and sea. Gullible sailors beware.

☐☐☐☐☐☐☐

9. Who, or what, came first into the kitchen?

☐☐☐

10. My nana makes a great impression.

☐☐☐☐

11. The rabbit sent a message to the guinea pig eons ago.

□□□□□□□

12. The tall bird, in a panic, ran erratically towards the water.

□□□□□

Answers on page 255.

WORD LADDER

Follow the clues and change one letter at a time to create a brand new word.

T R A Y

Set one of these to catch prey.

☐ ☐ ☐ ☐

To fall or a holiday.

☐ ☐ ☐ ☐

A firm one of these is important in a handshake and on a tennis racket.

☐ ☐ ☐ ☐

An oversized smile.

☐ ☐ ☐ ☐

Short for Grandma.

☐☐☐☐

A thousand of these in a kilo-

☐☐☐☐

To stuff in as much as you can.

☐☐☐☐

Found scuttling sideways on the shore.

☐☐☐☐

Dull-looking and uninteresting.

☐☐☐☐

Pull along behind.

☐☐☐☐

To boast about things you have done.

A spoiled child.

B	R	A	T

Answers on page 256.

PINDROP

- -

All of these words contain the word **PIN**. Use the clues to help you discover which words they are.

Example:

An evergreen tree which produces cones.

P	I	N	E

1. The group of bones that run down the back of an animal.

	P	I	N	

2. A mixture of white and red.

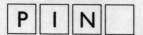

P	I	N	

3. Five hundred and sixty eight millilitres.

| P | I | N | |

4. Crabs, lobsters and scorpions have pairs of these.

| P | I | N | | | | |

5. People who hurt their legs or feet find it hard to walk without doing this.

| | | | P | I | N | |

6. Filled with candy and strung up high, this is fun to hit at a party.

| P | I | Ñ | | | |

7. Spikey fruit found on a Hawaiian pizza.

| P | I | N | | | | | |

8. Black and white rodent covered in sharp quills.

					P	I	N	

9. Turning around quickly.

	P	I	N

10. A person's view or judgement that isn't always based on fact.

	P	I	N			

11. Tall stories are best taken with one of these of salt.

P	I	N		

12. A small tortoise that prefers to live in freshwater.

					P	I	N

13. A nickname for the little finger.

| P | I | N | | |

14. Sleeping Beauty took a long nap after touching one of these.

| | P | I | N | | | |

Answers on page 256.

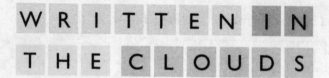

WRITTEN IN
THE CLOUDS

Look at these word clouds. Can you discover which book is contained in each cloud?

1.

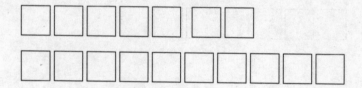

Mouse
Mushroom Caterpillar
Queen Hat Twins Head
Turtle Dinah Cat Door
RABBIT EAT ME Falling Mock
Heart Smile CAKE Nonsense
Curious CAKE Time Garden
White Tears LATE March Hare
Curiouser

2.

Sweets Chewing gum Little men
Television Chocolate bars
GLOOP Spoiled girl Greedy boy
Blueberry Salt Grandpa
Lifetime Ticket Gobstopper
Elevator Bucket Poor
Squirrel River

☐☐☐☐☐☐☐

☐☐☐☐☐

☐☐☐☐☐☐☐☐☐

☐☐☐☐☐☐☐

3. Barn Girl Winner
Shotgun Lives
Writing PiG Fair Rats
Prize Dies Fair Farmyard

☐☐☐☐☐☐☐☐☐☐☐

☐☐☐

27

4.

Magic
Evil School Scar Potions
Creatures Wand Professor
Headmaster House Hat Train Aunt
Platform GHOSTS Uncle Child
Alley Friends

☐☐☐☐☐

☐☐☐☐☐☐☐

☐☐☐☐☐☐

☐☐☐☐☐☐☐☐☐☐☐

5.

Apple Strawberry Moon Leaf Butterfly
Sausage Cupcake Watermelon Egg Lollipop
Pie Cheese Plums ICE CREAM

☐☐☐☐☐☐☐

☐☐☐☐☐

☐☐☐☐☐☐☐☐☐☐

Answers on page 256.

A MIX UP AT THE AIRPORT

Unscramble these mixed-up airport words. Have a safe flight!

Example:

CASUAL BOG REGGAE

B	A	G	G	A	G	E

C	A	R	O	U	S	E	L

I. TOPIARY RECRUITS

2. COP PATROLS SNORT

☐☐☐☐☐☐☐☐

☐☐☐☐☐☐☐

3. INKED CHECKS

☐☐☐☐☐ ☐☐

☐☐☐☐

4. SPURTED EAR

☐☐☐☐☐☐☐☐☐☐

5. LARS RIVA

☐☐☐☐☐☐☐☐

6. SNEER GAPS

[ ][ ][ ][ ][ ][ ][ ][ ][ ]

7. ARIAL LION PIT

[ ][ ][ ][ ][ ][ ][ ]
[ ][ ][ ][ ][ ]

8. FLATTEN THAT DING

[ ][ ][ ][ ][ ][ ]
[ ][ ][ ][ ][ ][ ][ ][ ][ ]

9. CAT ISSUE

[ ][ ][ ][ ][ ][ ][ ][ ]

31

10. UNWARY

☐☐☐☐☐☐

11. GAGGLE LOTUS

☐☐☐☐

☐☐☐☐☐☐☐

12. TYRE FEUD

☐☐☐☐ ☐☐☐☐

Answers on page 256.

GAMES GRID

Find the sports hidden in the grid below. Sports can be found in any direction, up, down, left right, diagonal as well as backwards and forwards.

O	K	E	D	F	X	S	O	P	Q
D	N	T	I	O	A	C	T	N	R
U	J	A	V	O	I	I	E	S	O
J	K	R	I	T	G	T	K	I	U
Y	Z	A	N	B	B	S	C	N	N
Z	E	K	G	A	M	A	I	N	D
K	N	K	L	L	Q	N	R	E	E
N	N	L	C	L	O	M	C	T	R
G	Z	X	I	O	X	Y	M	C	S
R	U	G	B	Y	H	G	F	H	E

FOOTBALL   CRICKET   GYMNASTICS
RUGBY   DIVING   NETBALL   HOCKEY
JUDO   TENNIS   KARATE   ROUNDERS

Answers on page 257.

A ll of the mythical beasts below fit in the grid. Can you work out where they go by counting the squares and using the number of letters in each word?

THREE LETTERS
ELF
IMP

FOUR LETTERS
OGRE
YETI
FAUN

FIVE LETTERS
FAIRY
GNOME
TROLL
HYDRA
SATYR

SIX LETTERS
DRAGON
GOBLIN
ZOMBIE
KELPIE
SELKIE

GORGON
SPHINX

SEVEN LETTERS
UNICORN
CYCLOPS
MERMAID
CENTAUR
GRIFFIN
PHOENIX
VAMPIRE

EIGHT LETTERS
MINOTAUR
WEREWOLF
BASILISK

NINE LETTERS

TEN LETTERS
LEPRECHAUN
HIPPOGRIFF

MYTHICAL BEAST

Answers on page 257.

35

CRYPTOGRAM CREATURES

Use the cipher below to complete these common phrases. Can you find which phrase is the odd one out and why?

A	B	C	D	E	F	G	H	I	J	K	L	M
Z	Y	X	W	V	U	T	S	R	Q	P	O	N

N	O	P	Q	R	S	T	U	V	W	X	Y	Z
M	L	K	J	I	H	G	F	E	D	C	B	A

1. URHS LFG LU DZGVI

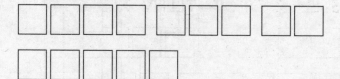

36

2. HMFT ZH Z YFT RM Z IFT

□□□□ □□ □

□□□ □□ □ □□□

3. GSV YLB DSL XIRVW DLOU

□□□ □□□ □□□

□□□□□ □□□□

4. HGIZRTSG UILN GSV SLIHVH
NLFGS

□□□□□□□□

□□□□ □□□

□□□□□□ □□□□□

5. LM Z DROW TLLHV XSZHV

□□ □ □□ □□

□□□□□□ □□□□□

37

6. OVG GSV XZG LFG LU GSV YZT

☐☐☐ ☐☐☐

☐☐☐ ☐☐☐

☐☐ ☐☐☐ ☐☐☐

7. TIZY GSW YFOO YB GSV SLIMH

☐☐☐☐ ☐☐☐

☐☐☐☐ ☐☐

☐☐☐ ☐☐☐☐

8. RM GSV WLT SLFHV

☐☐ ☐☐☐ ☐☐☐

☐☐☐☐☐

38

9. TLLW GSRMTH XLNV GL GSLHV
DSL DZRG

10. Z ORGGOV YRIW GLOW NV

11. GZPRMT GSV ORLMH HSZIV

12. WILKKRMT ORPV UORVH

39

13. PROO GDL YRIWH DRGS LME HGLMV

[   ][   ][   ][   ] [   ][   ][   ]

[   ][   ][   ][   ] [   ][   ][   ][   ]

[   ][   ][   ] [   ][   ][   ][   ][   ]

14. SLOW BLFI SLIHVH

[   ][   ][   ][   ] [   ][   ][   ][   ]

[   ][   ][   ][   ][   ]

The odd one out is number _____ because _____
_____.

Answers on page 258.

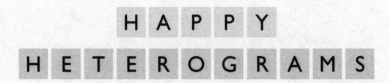

HAPPY HETEROGRAMS

A heterogram is a word in which each letter only appears once. Take a break and unscramble these heterograms.

Hint: pluck the grey petal from each flower and rearrange to give you a clue.

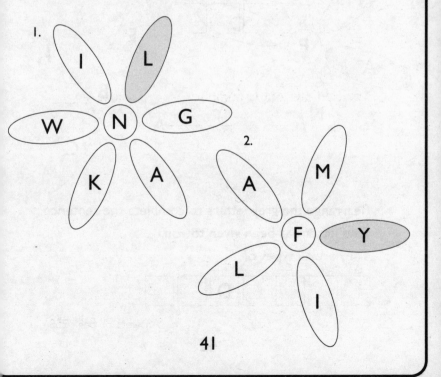

1.

2.

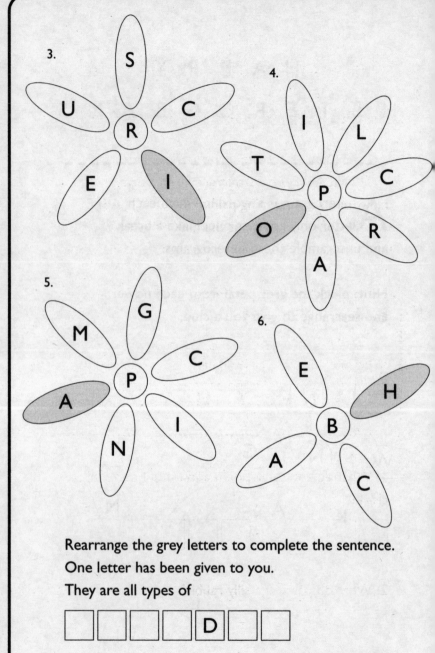

3.

S
U R C
E I

4.

I L
T P C
O R
A

5.

M G
A P C
N I

6.

E H
B
A C

Rearrange the grey letters to complete the sentence.

One letter has been given to you.

They are all types of

☐ ☐ ☐ ☐ D ☐ ☐

Answers on page 258.

- -

A hink pink is a rhyming pair of of ONE SYLLABLE words that answer a question. A hinky pinky is a rhyming pair of TWO SYLLABLE words. Can you work out the hink pinks AND hinky pinkies that answer these silly questions?

Example:

What do you call a dirty tissue?

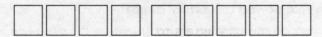

M A N K Y   H A N K Y

1. What do you call a poem about the hours on a clock?

☐ ☐ ☐ ☐   ☐ ☐ ☐ ☐

2. What do you call a silly rabbit?

☐☐☐☐☐ ☐☐☐☐☐

3. What do you call someone who steals
a novel from a shop?

☐☐☐☐☐ ☐☐☐☐☐

4. What's another name for funny facial hair?

☐☐☐☐☐ ☐☐☐☐☐

5. What do you call a hot drink that costs nothing?

☐☐☐☐ ☐☐☐

6. What do spooks have for Sunday lunch?

☐☐☐☐☐ ☐☐☐☐☐

7. What do you call a risky rumba?

☐☐☐☐☐☐

☐☐☐☐☐

8. What do you call a trembling turkey?

9. What do you call an American military vehicle?

10. What do you call a platter of seafood?

11. What do you call a monster's dinner?

12. What do you call a performance that lasts 24 hours?

13. What do you call something that gets on well with potatoes?

☐☐☐☐☐☐
☐☐☐☐☐

14. What do you call a very ordinary plug hole?

☐☐☐☐☐ ☐☐☐☐☐

15. What's another name for rubbish under the sea?

☐☐☐☐ ☐☐☐☐

16. What do you call a concealed mess?

☐☐☐☐☐☐
☐☐☐☐☐☐

17. What do you call a friendly discovery?

☐☐☐☐ ☐☐☐☐

18. What do you call a secret agent wrapped in pastry?

☐ ☐ ☐ ☐ ☐ ☐

19. What do you call a flower who won't get out of bed?

☐ ☐ ☐ ☐ ☐ ☐ ☐ ☐ ☐

20. What do you call a teacher's chest of drawers?

☐ ☐ ☐ ☐ ☐ ☐ ☐ ☐ ☐

☐ ☐ ☐ ☐ ☐ ☐ ☐

21. What do you call a pile of stuff that doesn't cost very much?

☐ ☐ ☐ ☐ ☐ ☐ ☐ ☐ ☐

Answers on pages 258-9.

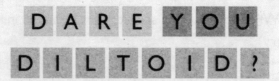

DARE YOU DILTOID?

A diltoid is a puzzle in which you are given clues that involve numbers and the initial letters of the word or words you need to find.

Example:

7 D ☐☐☐ in a W ☐☐☐

= 7 DAYS in a WEEK.

1. 52 C ☐☐☐☐☐ in a D ☐☐☐☐

2. 11 P ☐☐☐☐☐☐ in a

F ☐☐☐☐☐☐☐ T ☐☐☐

3. 9 L ☐☐☐☐ of a C ☐☐

4. 13 R ☐☐☐☐ in a
B ☐☐☐☐☐ D ☐☐☐☐

5. 2 S ☐☐☐☐ in a P ☐☐☐

6. 7 C ☐☐☐☐☐☐☐☐
in the W ☐☐☐☐

7. 366 D ☐☐☐ in a
L ☐☐☐ Y ☐☐☐

8. 12 S ☐ ☐ ☐ of the

Z ☐ ☐ ☐ ☐

9. 24 H ☐ ☐ ☐ ☐ in a D ☐ ☐

10. 8 P ☐ ☐ ☐ ☐ ☐ in the

S ☐ ☐ ☐ ☐ S ☐ ☐ ☐ ☐

11. 100 P ☐ ☐ ☐ ☐ ☐

in a P ☐ ☐ ☐

12. 7 C ☐ ☐ ☐ ☐ ☐ in a

R ☐ ☐ ☐ ☐ ☐

13. 26 L ☐☐☐☐☐☐ in the

A ☐☐☐☐☐☐☐

14. 288 P ☐☐☐☐

in this B ☐☐☐

Answers on page 259.

GOD ONE OUT

The gods on Mount Olympus have got themselves into a real muddle. Can you unscramble the supreme beings? Can you work out which god is the odd one out?

1. SUZE

☐ ☐ ☐ ☐

2. DENIS POO

☐ ☐ ☐ ☐ ☐ ☐ ☐ ☐

3. IRA STEM

☐ ☐ ☐ ☐ ☐ ☐ ☐

4. H RAE

☐ ☐ ☐ ☐

5. IDA THORPE

☐ ☐ ☐ ☐ ☐ ☐ ☐ ☐ ☐

6. SUSY DINO

☐ ☐ ☐ ☐ ☐ ☐ ☐ ☐

7. H R TO

☐ ☐ ☐ ☐

8. EM SHER

☐ ☐ ☐ ☐ ☐ ☐

9. PETE A SHUSH

☐ ☐ ☐ ☐ ☐ ☐ ☐ ☐ ☐ ☐

10. NATE HA

☐ ☐ ☐ ☐ ☐ ☐

11. ESRA

☐☐☐☐

12. AL POOL

☐☐☐☐☐☐

Answers on page 259.

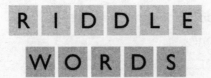

RIDDLE WORDS

Can you solve these wordy riddles?

1. What is the longest word in the dictionary?

2. Which word has five 'i's but if you have
it no one can see it?

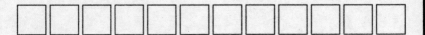

3. What do islands and the letter 'e' have in common?

□ □ □ □ □

4. Which three letter word must be broken before you can use it?

□ □ □

5. What must you keep when you give it to someone else?

□ □ □ □

6. Where can you find today always before yesterday and tomorrow?

□ □ □ □ □ □ □ □ □ □ □ □

Answers on page 259.

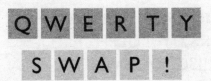

QWERTY SWAP!

As an April Fools' joke, the administrative assistant's teammates switched the keys on his computer from QWERTY to alphabetical order. Now he can't work what he typed when he took down everyone's lunch order. Can you work out what everyone is having and who the office joker is?

Q	W	E	R	T	Y	U	I	O	P
A	B	C	D	E	F	G	H	I	J

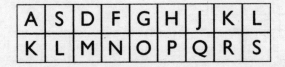

A	S	D	F	G	H	J	K	L
K	L	M	N	O	P	Q	R	S

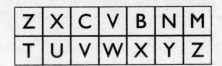

Z	X	C	V	B	N	M
T	U	V	W	X	Y	Z

57

1. **NCDPKE**
   LKSZIY LGLPH
   KJJSC QGHVC

2. **CSLK**
   EGDRCF BDQJ
   NDGHE LKSKM

3. DKH
EGYK KYM VGVGZXCD
LKYMBHVP SCZIYKMC

☐☐☐

☐☐☐☐ ☐☐☐

☐☐☐☐☐☐☐☐

☐☐☐☐☐☐☐☐

4. KYYK
KSJPKXCEEH LJKOPCEEH
LHSSF LZIIEPHC

☐☐☐☐

☐☐☐☐☐☐☐☐☐☐

☐☐☐☐☐☐☐☐

☐☐☐☐☐

☐☐☐☐☐☐☐☐

Answers on page 260.

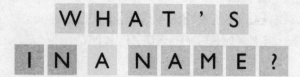
WHAT'S IN A NAME?

British athlete Keely Hodgkinson made a name for herself by breaking the British record in the women's 800 metres and taking home the silver medal at the Tokyo Olympic Games, but what can you make out of her name?

KEELY HODGKINSON

1. This captain was terrified of crocodiles.

☐☐☐☐

2. A small horse that looks a bit like an ass.

☐☐☐☐☐☐

3. Where Santa Claus hangs his bells.

☐☐☐☐☐☐

4. A great place to buy tickets in person.

☐☐☐☐☐

5. Place your eye here to sneak a peek.

☐☐☐☐☐☐

6. Of Mirren or of Troy.

☐☐☐☐☐

7. You can build with these or break a grownups foot.

☐☐☐☐

8. All the best stories have a happy one.

☐☐☐☐☐☐

9. For blinking or winking, you will need at least one of these.

☐☐☐☐☐☐

10. A fine fabric made from worm cocoons.

☐☐☐☐

11. Most people are born with two of these.
A chilli would be nothing without the beans.

☐☐☐☐☐☐

12. Beloved by bears, sweet before badger or bee.

☐☐☐☐☐

13. The thirty-fifth president of the United States.

☐☐☐☐☐☐☐

14. There's nothing funny about the yellow part of an egg.

☐☐☐☐

15. A way of being injured by someone's leg.

☐☐☐☐☐

16. A famous story from the past that we can be sure is true.

☐☐☐☐☐☐

17. What do angry people behind the wheel, fancy cheeses, and geese all have in common?

☐☐☐☐☐☐☐

Answers on page 260.

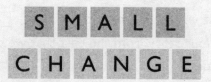

SMALL CHANGE

With a small change a word in each of these clues can take on a whole new meaning. Can you add, take away, twist and turn the letters to create a new word?

Example:

Without a twist in <u>Spain</u>

S	P	I	N

1. Turning words into a weapon.

2. The thorn on the rose made her finger.

3. Hello story! It's in the past.

☐☐☐☐☐☐☐

4. The last fish in all the seas.

☐☐☐☐☐

5. The trick lost I in my coin.

☐☐☐

6. Where mixed stew was enjoyed in the wild.

☐☐☐☐

7. The first sun made the team hot under the collar.

☐☐☐☐☐

8. Her win blew them all away.

☐☐☐☐

9. Their wins proved they were evenly matched.

[ ][ ][ ][ ][ ]

10. Her accident left pills all over the floor.

[ ][ ][ ][ ][ ]

Answers on page 260.

HIDDEN HORRORS

Find the hidden terrors lurking within these spooky sentences.

Can you find the odd one out?

Example:

Ghosts care deeply about how they make you feel.

Ghosts <u>care d</u>eeply about how they make you feel.

S	C	A	R	E	D

---

1. If you go for a hike or a stroll, be sure to look carefully under the bridge.

2. Beware the elephant omens.

☐☐☐☐☐☐☐

3. Leaving hosts without bidding farewell is an impolite way to say goodbye.

☐☐☐☐☐☐

4. After her death my rich aunt sometimes visited me in the night.

☐☐☐☐☐

5. The spectre at the ghoulish gala only liked desserts.

☐☐☐☐☐

6. The medium learned that only a rare ape recoils from the figure of death.

☐☐☐☐☐☐

7. The mad scientist split the atom because he wanted a fast track to the afterlife.

☐☐☐☐

8. A safe place to sleep is a basic ask eternal.

☐☐☐☐☐☐

9. The wizard knew he needed to cast a spell now and that it had better be good.

☐☐☐☐

10. A sleepless night made Monday difficult.

☐☐☐☐☐

11. The giant was no match against the witch.

☐☐☐

12. To escape the curse of the pharoah's tomb cry, "Ptolemy the Great!"

☐☐☐☐☐

Answers on page 260.

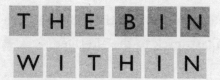

THE BIN WITHIN

Each of the words below have the word **BIN** within them. Can you work out what these words are? Use the clues to help you.

Example:

Shout out the name of this game when you complete your grid.

| B | I | N | G | O |

1. A home, sometimes made of logs and found in the woods.

| | | B | I | N |

2. Wind this up with plenty thread.

| | | | B | I | N |

3. To eat or watch too much of a good thing.

| B | I | N | | |

4. Turned by wind or water, this can generate power.

| | | | B | I | N | |

5. A cupboard in your kitchen, or bathroom.

| | | B | I | N | | |

6. Hold a pair of these to eyes to help you see things that are far away.

| B | I | N | | | | | | | |

7. Riding down a river or a mountain on a rubber ring.

		B	I	N	

8. Keep your papers together in a ring one of these.

B	I	N			

9. Singing bird with red chest feathers.

		B	I	N

Answers on pages 260-1.

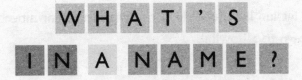

WHAT'S IN A NAME?

British football player Marcus Rashford has made a name for himself both on and off the pitch, but what can you make out of his name? Use the clues to find the words hidden in the letters of his name.

MARCUS RASHFORD

1. City in the northeast of England on the banks of the River Wear.

☐ ☐ ☐ ☐ ☐ ☐

2. Trees filled with fruit grow here.

☐ ☐ ☐ ☐ ☐ ☐ ☐

3. Join in for the catchy bit of a song.

☐ ☐ ☐ ☐ ☐ ☐

4. Little Miss Muffet likes nothing more than sitting down to a bowlful.

☐☐☐☐☐

5. All the food for school lunches is grown on one of these

☐☐☐☐

6. A national dish when served with chips.

☐☐☐

7. Island in the northwest of Greece.

☐☐☐☐☐

8. Small blue people with white hats.

☐☐☐☐☐☐

9. Sing, but with your lips together.

☐☐☐

10. A broken piece of glass or metal that towers over London Bridge.

☐ ☐ ☐ ☐ ☐

11. Romans held their meetings here.

☐ ☐ ☐ ☐ ☐

12. Swampy wetland covered in plants.

☐ ☐ ☐ ☐ ☐

13. Pulses of electromagnetic rays that can tell you where things are.

☐ ☐ ☐ ☐ ☐

14. Whether on a wave or the web, you'll never be bored.

☐ ☐ ☐ ☐

15. Between three and five members in a quartet.

☐ ☐ ☐ ☐

16. A large gap between two rocks or ways of thinking.

☐ ☐ ☐ ☐ ☐

17. A serious performance on stage or screen.

☐ ☐ ☐ ☐ ☐

18. Fancy shop in Knightsbridge, London.

☐ ☐ ☐ ☐ ☐ ☐ ☐

Answers on page 261.

SEEING THE WOOD FOR THE TREES

Can you find all the trees in this word search? While you are among the trees, see if you can find Robin Hood's favourite forest?

O	H	A	W	T	H	O	R	N	Y
C	P	A	A	S	F	B	S	K	E
H	L	P	L	H	I	E	Y	W	W
E	A	O	N	E	R	E	C	I	C
S	N	P	U	R	B	C	A	L	E
T	E	L	T	W	O	H	M	L	D
N	P	A	E	O	X	O	O	O	A
U	I	R	L	O	A	L	R	W	R
T	N	N	M	D	S	L	E	F	H
P	E	D	T	B	H	Y	O	A	K

All the trees are listed on the next page.

OAK

ELM

CEDAR

YEW

HAWTHORN

PLANE

SYCAMORE

WALNUT

WILLOW

CHESTNUT

HOLLY

PINE

BEECH

ASH

FIR

BOX

POPLAR

BONUS FOREST

				W	O	O	D

Answers on page 261.

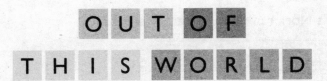

OUT OF THIS WORLD

U nscramble the initial letters of the words in these sentences to find the space words.

Example:

Ian read just enough pages to understand.

<u>I</u>an <u>r</u>ead <u>j</u>ust <u>e</u>nough <u>p</u>ages <u>t</u>o <u>u</u>nderstand.

I	R	J	E	P	T	U

J	U	P	I	T	E	R

1. Always make your legs kick you when idle.

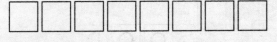

2. As Nora ran she uncovered termites.

3. How can anyone like kale, especially on lamb burgers?

4. Next door's dog ate my aunt's red dahlias over Easter.

5. A space cadet on Saturn took pains not to irritate every alien.

Answers on page 261.

WORD LADDER

Transform **BAKE** into the word **CARE** one letter at a time. Follow the clues and fill in answers. Each answer is one letter different to the one before.

B	A	K	E

Vehicle with two wheels.

When you don't quite love it.

A sour, green citrus fruit.

Act without words.

☐☐☐☐

Measured by a clock.

☐☐☐☐

Take something wild and make it friendly.

☐☐☐☐

A sticky strip that comes on a roll.

☐☐☐☐

A coat without sleeves.

☐☐☐☐

Look after someone you love.

C A R E

Answers on page 261.

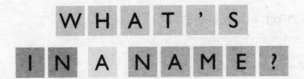

British pop icon Harry Styles first made a name for himself on a TV talent show – The X Factor, but what can you make out of his name?

HARRY STYLES

1. A pet in the street with no home.

☐ ☐ ☐ ☐ ☐

2. Have a go, or make an effort.

☐ ☐ ☐

3. Four on a car and two on a bike? Sounds exhausting.

☐ ☐ ☐ ☐ ☐

4. After a busy day you need to.

☐ ☐ ☐ ☐

5. In Russia they had no kings but twisted rats.

☐ ☐ ☐ ☐

6. What chips and the ocean have in common.

☐ ☐ ☐ ☐ ☐

7. What do you get when you are on your marks?

☐ ☐ ☐

8. For some ridiculous reason, drawing these on anything makes them a girl.

☐ ☐ ☐ ☐ ☐ ☐

9. It's a wonder that big ones shine and little ones twinkle.

☐ ☐ ☐ ☐

10. Feeling itchy at the last minute.

☐ ☐ ☐ ☐

11. Electric car that parks itself in space.

☐ ☐ ☐ ☐ ☐

12. Scarce bloody steak.

☐ ☐ ☐ ☐

13. As a fox.

☐ ☐ ☐

14. It's not his, theirs or xyrs? It's...

☐ ☐ ☐ ☐

15. Is Stephenson strictly a children's presenter?

☐ ☐ ☐ ☐

Answers on page 262.

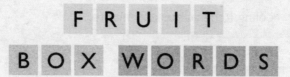

FRUIT BOX WORDS

This grid contains five delicious fruits. The first letter of each fruit can be found in column one, the second in column two etc. Can you find all five of the hidden fruits?

	1	2	3	4	5
	M	P	A	P	H
	P	R	P	O	E
	A	E	A	L	N
	G	E	M	O	N
	L	E	L	C	E

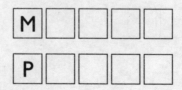

86

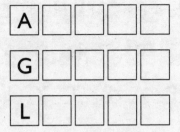

Answers on page 262.

THE RUNED BIRTHDAY PARTY!

Jamie loves history, especially Viking history. To celebrate their love of history, and their birthday, Jamie wrote their invitations in runes.

Can you help the guests work out where and when the birthday party is so that Jamie's birthday isn't ruined in more ways than one?

A	B	C	D	E	F	G	H	I	J	K	L	M
ᚠ	ᛒ	ᚲ	ᛞ	ᛗ	ᚡ	ᚷ	ᚺ	ᛁ	ᛇ	ᚴ	ᛚ	ᛖ

N	O	P	Q	R	S	T	U	V	W	X	Y	Z
ᛏ	ᛟ	ᛈ	ᚲ	ᚱ	ᛋ	ᛏ	ᚢ	ᛈ	ᚹ	ᛉ	ᛃ	ᛦ

WHERE:

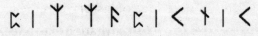

□ □ □   □ □ □ □ □

□ □ □ □ □ □

WHAT:

□ □ □ □ □   □ □ □ □ □ □

WHEN:
1 p.m.

□ □ □ □ □ □ □ □

BRING:

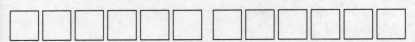

□ □ □ □ □ □ □ □ □ □ □

Answers on page 262.

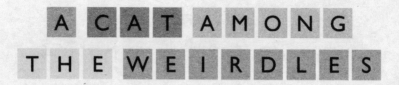

A CAT AMONG THE WEIRDLES

All of the words below contain the word **CAT**. Use the clues to help you lo**CAT**e these words.

> **Example:**
>
> Cows and bulls for milk and meat.
>
> **C A T T L E**

1. This flashing light on a vehicle lets you know where it is going.

2. To throw all over the place.

| | C | A | T | | | |

3. A short sleep during the day.

| C | A | T | | | |

4. What does a teacher do?

| | | | C | A | T | |

5. A magazine in which everything comes at a cost.

| C | A | T | | | | | | |

6. You would have to find this on a map.

| | | C | A | T | | | |

7. A saying a person is known for using a lot.

| C | A | T | | | | | | | | |

8. A favourite weapon of ancient armies, used for hurling things at castles and cavalry.

| C | A | T | | | | | |

9. In the USA people take one of these instead of a holiday.

| | | C | A | T | | | |

Answers on page 262.

A hinky pinky is a rhyming pair of of TWO SYLLABLE words that answer a question. A hink pink is a rhyming pair of ONE SYLLABLE words. Can you work out the hinky pinkies AND hink pinks that answer these silly questions?

Example:

What do you call the sad face someone pulls when they see round green vegetables?

| S | P | R | O | U | T | | P | O | U | T |

1. What do you call an obstacle made from sour milk?

| C | U | R | D | L | E |

| H | U | R | D | L | E |

2. What do you call a run with your canine friend?

| D | O | G | | J | O | G |

3. What do you call a stack of folders?

| F | I | L | E | | P | I | L | E |

4. What do you call a shovel larger than the one you have?

| B | I | G | G | E | R |

| D | I | G | G | E | R |

5. What do you call an enormous canal boat?

| L | A | R | G | E | | B | A | R | G | E |

6. The best trailer in a parade that the world has ever seen.

| | | | | | | | |

FLOAT?

7. What do you call high quality salt water from a tin of tuna?

F I N E B R I N E

8. What do you call a tan tiara?

B R O W N C R O W N

9. What do you call a spicy yellow dessert topping?

M U S T A R D
C U S T A R D

10. What do you call someone who isn't as good at looking for things as someone else?

☐ ☐ ☐ ☐ ☐
☐ ☐ ☐ ☐ ☐

11. What do you have when you have picked up 100 lucky pennies?

F O U N D P O U N D

95

12. What do you call a wearable clock with a tartan strap?

S C O T C H
W A T C H

13. What do you call a young cat that's in love?

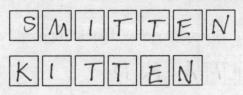

S M I T T E N
K I T T E N

14. What do you call a truck that feels it has to apologize?

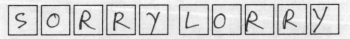

S O R R Y   L O R R Y

15. What do you call someone who takes all the foliage from your garden?

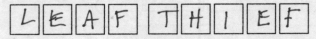

L E A F   T H I E F

Answers on page 262.

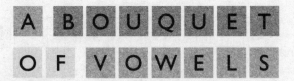

A BOUQUET
OF VOWELS

The florist's ordering system has come down with a case of sticky vowel virus. Can you fill in the missing vowels and complete the order for the bouquet?

A E I O U

> **Example:**
>
> | R | | S | |
> |---|---|---|---|
> | R | O | S | E |

1. | D | | | S | Y |
   |---|---|---|---|---|

2. | L | | L | Y |
   |---|---|---|---|

3. | C | | R | N | | T | | | N |

4. | | R | | S |

5. | T | | L | | P |

6. | | N | | M | | N | |

7. | P | | P | P | Y |

8. | P | | | N | Y |

9. | D | | N | D | | L | | | N |

10.  V □ □ L □ T

11.  D □ F F □ D □ L

Can you spot which flower you would be unlikely to find in a bouquet?

Answers on page 263.

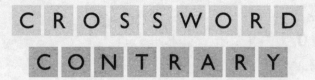

CROSSWORD CONTRARY

F ill in the crossword with each of the clue's opposites. Number one has been done for you!

ACROSS

3. White
5. Wrong
7. Tight
9. Country
10. Rise
12. Up
13. Cat
15. On
17. Soft
19. Before
22. Leave
23. You
24. Break

DOWN

1. In
2. Death
3. Sharp
4. Fast
6. Cold
8. Large
10. Lose
11. High
14. Bad
16. Near
18. Dangerous
20. Dim
21. Go
24. Break

Answers on page 263.

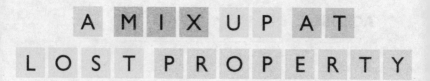

A MIX UP AT LOST PROPERTY

There has been a mix up at the lost property at the railway station. Can you help unscramble the mess?

Example:

JET CAK

J A C K E T

1. BLAH BOBET

2. CODE FAT FLU

3. CARL RAID

□□□□□□□□

4. NICORATA

□□□□□□□□

5. CAPABLE SLAB

□□□□□□□□

□□□

6. LURE BALM

□□□□□□□□

7. ARTIST HEWS

□□□□□□□□□□

8. UK CRACKS

☐☐☐☐☐☐☐☐

9. FRISBEE CA

☐☐☐☐☐☐☐☐☐

10. EVILNESS FLOGGERS

☐☐☐☐☐☐☐☐☐☐

☐☐☐☐☐☐

Answers on page 263.

A MIGHTY DIN

All of these words have the word **DIN**. Use the clues to help you.

1. A species of dog found in Australia.

D I N ☐ ☐

2. Nothing strange about this word.

☐ ☐ D I N ☐ ☐ ☐

3. A terrible lizard from long ago.

D I N ☐ ☐ ☐ ☐ ☐

4. His lamp will grant his wishes.

| | | | | D | I | N |

5. This game fish comes crushed in a tin.

| | | | D | I | N | |

6. An inflatable boat you can take to the beach.

| D | I | N | | | |

7. A way of looking after your own business.

| | | | D | I | N | |

Answers on page 263.

Look at these word clouds. Can you discover which film is contained within each cloud?

I.

Chimney Medicine Fun
Umbrella Brother Two pence
Sister NANNY Kite Wind
Sugar Invest Birds
London Practically
Bank Mother
Atrocious Father Work Perfect
Impossible PARK
Letter Precocious Horse race
Advertisement Bag
Spoonful

2.

True Ice Love Forget
MAGIC Snowman Reindeer Sled
Castle Sauna Princess Queen
Spirits Betrayal Secret Troll
Fixer Winter Ball Shipwreck
Coronation Summer
Never Cold Prince Heart
Kiss

☐ ☐ ☐ ☐ ☐ ☐

3.

Koala Contest Collapse
JELLYFISH Pig Mum Theatre
Elephant Aquarium
Prize Lizard Gorilla Porcupine
Piglets Competition Rehearsal Rock
Dream Father bottom Rubble Flood
Show MONEY
Prison Escape Piano

☐ ☐ ☐ ☐

4.

Tired **Pumpkin** *Halloween*

Presents **Mad** **Scientist** SECRET

Sleigh Kidnap

Scary **Toys** *Frightened* Missiles

Santa **Boys** **Girls** *Bogeyman*

HOLIDAY

Celebrate **Trick or Treat** *Henchman*

Bugs Ghost

Witches Graveyard Dog

Laboratory Square MAYOR

Casino

Town *Sack* **King** Forest

Trees **Castle** DOORS

<table>
<tr><td></td><td></td><td></td></tr>
</table>

<table>
<tr><td></td><td></td><td></td><td></td><td></td><td></td><td></td><td></td><td></td></tr>
</table>

<table>
<tr><td></td><td></td><td></td><td></td><td></td><td></td><td></td></tr>
</table>

<table>
<tr><td></td><td></td><td></td><td></td><td></td><td></td><td></td><td></td></tr>
</table>

Answers on page 264.

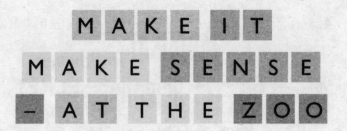

MAKE IT MAKE SENSE – AT THE ZOO

Each of the following statements contains one word that makes it too weird to be true. Can you replace one word in each of sentences to make it make sense?

Example:

Elephants have big ears long trousers.

Elephants have big ears long ~~trousers~~.

Elephants have big ears long <u>TRUNKS</u>.

110

1. Some arachnids such as spiders spin tunes to trap their prey.

| W | | | |

2. Animals that eat both plants and other animals are called omnipotent.

| O | M | N | I | | O | | | |

3. Panda bears can eat up to forty kilograms of bambino in a single day.

| B | | | | | |

4. Sir Attenborough is famous for making documentaries about animation.

| A | | | | A | | |

5. In the middle ages, doctors put lemurs on people's wounds to draw out the blood.

| L | | | | | | |

6. Animals that eat meat are called carnivals.

| C | | | | | | | |

7. The bald earthworm is the national symbol of the United States of America.

| E | | | | |

8. Animals that can breathe both on land and in water are known as amphitheatres.

| A | M | P | H | | | | A | | |

9. Contractors are type non-venomous snake who crush their prey with their strong bodies.

| C | O | N | | | | | C | | O | |

10. Flying squiggles live in trees and have parachute-like skin between their legs to help them glide.

| S | | | | | | | | |

11. The Neanderthal is a medium-sized whale with a elongated tooth sticking out of its head like a unicorn.

N						

Answers on page 264.

Transform **BARN** into the word **FIRE** one letter at a time. Follow the clues and fill in answers. Each answer is one letter different to the one before.

| B | A | R | N |

When a dog wants your attention.

| | | | |

A place to keep your money.

| | | | |

A ship at the bottom of the ocean.

| | | | |

114

Stand here to brush your teeth.

☐☐☐☐

A cheeky blink with one eye only.

☐☐☐☐

Connect two or more things together.

☐☐☐☐

Draw it. Cross it. Hang washing on it.

☐☐☐☐

Perfectly adequate or of high quality.

☐☐☐☐

| F | I | R | E |

Answers on page 264.

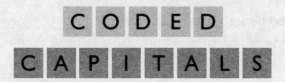

CODED CAPITALS

There's been a mix up at MI5. Important boxes addressed in Morse code are missing letters, can you help work out which capital cities these messages need to be sent to?

See if you can work out which countries each of these cities are in. Some you may know, for the others use the code to help.

MORSE CODE

A	B	C	D	E	F	G	H	I	J	K	L	M
•-	-•••	-•-•	-••	•	••-•	--•	••••	••	•---	-•-	•-••	--

N	O	P	Q	R	S	T	U	V	W	X	Y	Z
-•	---	•--•	--•-	•-•	•••	-	••-	•••-	•--	-••-	-•--	--••

Example:

P	A	R	I	S

		A			E

F	R	A	N	C	E

I.

						A	

	A		A	I		A

117

2.

•--	•-	•••	••••	••	-•	--•	-	---	-•	--•	-•-•

	•••	
U		A

3.

-•••	•	•-•	•-••	••	-•

--•		•-•	--		-•	-•--
	E			A		

118

4.

[seven empty boxes]

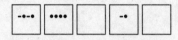

[empty] [empty] | I | A

5.

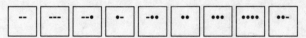

[nine empty boxes]

[empty] | O | [empty] | A | [empty] | I | A

119

6.

| -.- | -.-- | .. | .... |

| | | | |

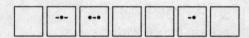

| | -.- | .-- | | | -. | |

| U | | | A | I | | E |

7.

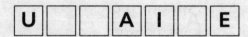

| -.. | .... | .- | -.- | .- |

| | | | | |

| -... | | -. | --. | .-.. | | -.. | | ... | .... |

| | A | | | A | | E | | | |

Answers on page 264.

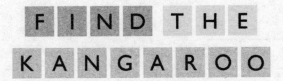

FIND THE KANGAROO

A kangaroo word is a word that contains a shorter synonym (word with a similar meaning) to itself. This synonym is called a 'joey'. In order to be a true kangaroo word, the letters of the joey have to be in the correct order. Look at the joey words below and see if you can figure out their kangaroo words.

Example:

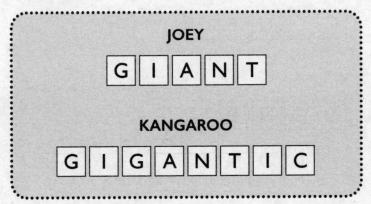

JOEY

G I A N T

KANGAROO

G I G A N T I C

1.

| A | T | E |

| | | A | | T | E | |

2.

| I | S |

| | | I | S | | |

3.

| C | U | E |

| C | | U | E |

4.

| L | O | N | E |

| | L | O | N | E |

122

5.

| B | U | S | T |

| B | U | | S | T |

6.

| C | L | E | A | N |

| C | L | E | A | N | | |

7.

| S | A | D |

| | | S | | A | | D |

8.

| S | L | I | D |

| S | L | I | | | | | D |

9.

10.

Answers on page 264.

MIXED-UP FAIRY TALES

- -

Each of these mixed up words and phrases conceals a famous fairy tale. Unscramble the letters to fill in the boxes below.

1. ENDANGERS LETHAL

	A			L

A	N	D					L

2. ERIN CALLED

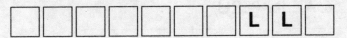

						L	L	

3. TIPSY BUNGEE ALE

| | | E | E | | | | |

| | E | | | | | |

4. BISON SPOUTS

| | | S | S | | |

| | | | | S |

5. PRINTED ACNE SHAPES

| P | | | | | | S | S |

| | | | | | | P | |

6. AZ IN PERU

| R | | | | | Z | | |

7. SWOT WHINE

| S | | | | | H | | | |

8. DEIDRE TO DO THRILLING

| | | T | T | | | R | | |

| R | | | | | | | | |

Answers on page 265.

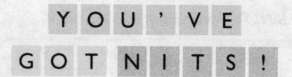

YOU'VE GOT NITS!

Each of the words below have the word **NIT** within them. Can you work out what these words are? Use the clues to help you.

Example:

To bring two or more things together.

U	N	I	T	E

1. The first letters in your first and last name.

	N	I	T				

2. Use needles and yarn and do this to make a sweater.

	N	I	T				

3. To set on fire.

		N	I	T	

4. Unlimited. To go on forever.

				N	I	T	

5. Volcanic rock used to make kitchen worktops and buildings.

			N	I	T	

6. To keep a watch on something or the screen on a computer.

		N	I	T		

7. Gas that makes up 70% of the earth atmosphere.

| N | I | T | | | | |

8. Hiding who you really are.

| | | | | | N | I | T | |

9. A person who tells tales.

| | N | I | T | | |

10. The people who live around you in your local area.

| | | | | N | I | T | |

Answers on page 265.

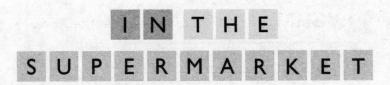

Find the missing vowels to complete these common supermarket items. Some are easier than others!

A E I O U

Example:

BRKFST CRL

| B | R | E | A | K | F | A | S | T |

| C | E | R | E | A | L |

131

1. YGHRT

▢▢▢▢▢▢▢

2. CHDDRCHS

▢▢▢▢▢▢▢

▢▢▢▢▢▢

3. PPLS

▢▢▢▢▢▢

4. RNGS

▢▢▢▢▢▢▢

5. BRD

▢▢▢▢▢

132

6. PTTS

<table>
<tr><td> </td><td> </td><td> </td><td> </td><td> </td><td> </td><td> </td><td> </td></tr>
</table>

7. CHCLTBSCTS

<table>
<tr><td> </td><td> </td><td> </td><td> </td><td> </td><td> </td><td> </td><td> </td><td> </td></tr>
</table>

<table>
<tr><td> </td><td> </td><td> </td><td> </td><td> </td><td> </td><td> </td><td> </td></tr>
</table>

8. BKDBNS

<table>
<tr><td> </td><td> </td><td> </td><td> </td><td> </td><td> </td><td> </td><td> </td><td> </td><td> </td></tr>
</table>

9. SPGHTT

<table>
<tr><td> </td><td> </td><td> </td><td> </td><td> </td><td> </td><td> </td><td> </td><td> </td></tr>
</table>

10. TMTS

<table>
<tr><td> </td><td> </td><td> </td><td> </td><td> </td><td> </td><td> </td><td> </td></tr>
</table>

11. NNS

☐☐☐☐☐☐

12. LTTC

☐☐☐☐☐☐☐

13. DGHNTS

☐☐☐☐☐☐☐☐☐

14. CCMBR

☐☐☐☐☐☐☐☐

15. FRZNPZZ

☐☐☐☐☐☐ ☐☐☐☐☐

16. SWTCRN

☐☐☐☐☐☐☐☐☐

17. BTTR

☐☐☐☐☐☐

18. STRWBYJM

☐☐☐☐☐☐☐☐☐☐

☐☐☐

19. CHCKN

☐☐☐☐☐☐☐

Answers on page 265.

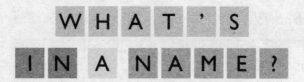

WHAT'S IN A NAME?

US singer, songwriter and actress Ariana Grande first made a name for herself as an actress before becoming a multi award-winning music megastar, but what can you make out of her name?

ARIANA GRANDE

1. It's the first colour in the rainbow, Richard!

☐☐☐

2. These items of jewellery are usually found in pairs and come in pierced or clip on versions.

☐☐☐☐☐☐☐

3. People who live in houses sometimes have front and back ones of these – great for planting flowers and vegetables.

☐☐☐☐☐☐

4. Group of three waterfalls found in New York State, USA.

☐☐☐☐☐☐☐

5. Princess/Lady. Mother of Princes William and Harry.

☐☐☐☐☐

6. It is well chronicled that you will need to go through the back of a wardrobe to enter this magical land.

☐☐☐☐☐☐

7. Rice, corn, oats and wheat are all forms of this food.

☐☐☐☐☐

8. To rule. Queen Elizabeth II's has been record-breaking!

☐☐☐☐☐

9. To make coffee or flour, you need to do this first!

☐☐☐☐☐

10. Breakfast, lunch and this meal make up your three meals a day.

☐☐☐☐☐☐

11. A feel-good film or book has a happy one.

☐☐☐☐☐☐

12. This system uses radio waves to locate and detect things that cannot be seen.

☐☐☐☐☐

13. To understand this clue, you need to be able to do this.

☐ ☐ ☐ ☐

14. Warning signs let you know when you are approaching this. Some people like to think it is their middle name.

☐ ☐ ☐ ☐ ☐ ☐

15. To organize things or make plans. Some people do it with flowers.

☐ ☐ ☐ ☐ ☐ ☐ ☐

Answers on page 265.

WORD LADDER

- -

Follow the clues and change one letter at a time to create a brand new word.

Of great height.

☐ ☐ ☐ ☐

At the end of the spine. Some animals wag theirs when they are happy.

☐ ☐ ☐ ☐

Knock one of these of the stumps in cricket or pay it to get out of jail.

☐ ☐ ☐ ☐

Cry very loudly.

☐☐☐☐

Life is one of these filled with cherries.

☐☐☐☐

Tie ribbons in your hair or around gifts into these.

☐☐☐☐

They give us milk.

☐☐☐☐

Pigeons, doves and happy babies make these sounds.

☐☐☐☐

Unless you want food raw, you need to learn how
to do this.

☐☐☐☐

Turn its pages or make a reservation.

☐☐☐☐

Knee high or ankle, the Duke of Wellington loved them.

☐☐☐☐

The sound of an owl at night or a laugh.

☐☐☐☐

A hula ring to keep around your middle.

☐☐☐☐

Make one of these to make a knot.

L O O P

Answers on page 266.

BOX WORDS

This grid contains four farm animals each with four letters. The first letter of each animal can be found in column one, the second in column two etc. Can you find all four of the farm animals?

	1	2	3	4
	L	U	L	F
	G	A	M	K
	D	O	A	B
	C	A	C	K

L □ □ □

G □ □ □

D □ □ □

C □ □ □

BONUS CLUE: two animals are babies.

Answers on page 266.

WEIRDSEARCH – ANIMALS DOWN UNDER

Take a trip to Australia and New Zealand to find some curious creatures. Look up any animals you haven't heard of before.

W	U	K	Q	P	J	L	S	E	D	M	M
A	T	I	P	L	L	U	C	A	U	U	U
L	Q	W	Q	O	P	H	L	T	G	S	P
L	L	I	U	Y	I	A	K	C	O	S	T
A	I	Q	T	D	H	O	W	P	N	O	O
B	K	A	N	G	A	R	O	O	G	P	O
Y	L	A	R	L	W	O	M	B	A	T	C
P	F	I	A	E	E	U	T	Y	N	G	I
H	M	C	N	T	D	M	Y	W	U	A	D
D	I	N	G	O	S	I	U	P	K	L	N
R	H	S	I	F	Y	L	L	E	J	A	A
P	E	L	I	C	A	N	Z	G	Q	H	B

KOALA

KANGAROO

DINGO

PLATYPUS

WOMBAT

ECHIDNA

DUGONG

GLIDER

EMU

KIWI

BANDICOOT

JELLYFISH

WALLABY

POSSUM

PELICAN

QUOLL

GALAH

Answers on page 266.

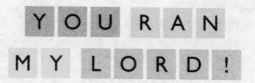

YOU **RAN**
MY LO **RD**!

Each of the words below have the word **RAN** within them. Can you work out what these words are? Use the clues to help you.

Example:

The seventh planet in the solar system.

U R A N U S

1. Someone you don't know, who you probably shouldn't speak to.

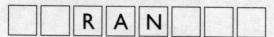

☐ ☐ R A N ☐ ☐ ☐

2. Your mother or father's mother.

	R	A	N						

3. Flesh-eating fish found in the rivers and lakes of South America.

		R	A	N		

4. The level a person has reached in the army or police force.

R	A	N	

5. Long-legged water bird.

	R	A	N	

6. Country south of the United Kingdom famous for its bread and cheese.

	R	A	N		

7. Play a practical joke on someone.

	R	A	N	

8. A mixture of red and yellow, nothing rhymes with this sweet citrus.

	R	A	N		

9. Arranged in no particular order.

R	A	N			

10. Dried black fruit in a bun.

			R	A	N	

11. Furry purse worn with a kilt.

				R	A	N

12. Buses, cars, trains and taxis are all forms of this.

	R	A	N					

13. A person who sings with a high voice.

			R	A	N	

14. Firefighters can connect their hoses to one of these.

			R	A	N	

15. Make a grand one through the front door.

			R	A	N		

16. This sour red fruit makes the perfect Christmas sauce.

	R	A	N					

17. Enormous hairy spider, thought to eat birds.

| | | R | A | N | | | | |

18. Fancy or fast food, they serve food here.

| | | | | | | R | A | N | |

19. A part of a tree.

| | R | A | N | | |

20. The skull.

| | R | A | N | | | |

Answers on page 266.

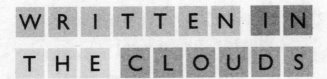

WRITTEN IN THE CLOUDS

Look at these word clouds. Can you discover which classic children's book is contained within each cloud?

1.
Never
Fairy WiNG
Crocodile Clock
Fly **Pirate**
Lost **Boy** Darling Hook
Darling **Captain** Crying
Wendy **Captain**
Kensington **Nana** Michael
Window Nursery Rings *Bell*
pixie dust

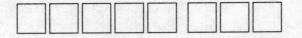

2.

Enchantress

Winter Lamp post Beaver

Fur coat Fawn Edmund

Evacuees Susan

Children

Lucy Snow Peter WOLVES

Turkish delight Stone table beasts

Good EVIL Spring

Tumnus Pevensie

Cair Paravel Queen centaur

shield

Aslan sword bow

ARROWS horn

dagger

ointment

3.

teddy RABBIT
pig donkey owl robin
kangaroo tiger
honey WOOD tree
bees stuck
woozle balloon footprints
jar Heffalump tail sticks
river message
bridge bath
birthday visiting bottle
friends

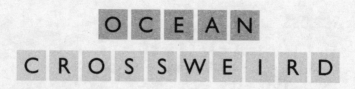

OCEAN CROSSWEIRD

Do these clues to this crossword look a bit weird? That's because they include the answers scrambled in CAPITAL LETTERS. Unscramble the letters to help you complete this cryptic cross weird.

154

ACROSS

1. The largest mammals in the ocean come from the **HAWEL** family.

9. Turtles love to eat stinging **JILLY SHEF**.

10. Fish and mammals of all sizes eat **KONPLANT** soup.

12. Clownfish hide among the tentacles of **NEENOMA**

14. A **FEFFURSHIP** can expand to three times there ordinary size when scared.

17. Beware the nip of the sideways scuttling **CARB**.

18. **HISFARTS** are stellar and can have between five and fifty legs.

20. **ARCOL** is an architect of the ocean, building reefs, walls and caves.

22. Intelligent, eight-limbed ocean molluscs – **CUTSPOO**.

24. Giddy up riding a **SEASHORE**.

25. **POLLSAC** shells scoot across the ocean floor.

26. Fish, birds and ocean mammals love to eat tiny shrimp called **LRILK**.

27. A cone-shelled **ELMPIT** clings to the rocks.

More clues on the next page.

DOWN

2. **BOLSTER** have claws and live on the ocean floor.

3. **ANGRYSIT** is a flat fish have a venomous barb in its tail.

4. A friendly **HIDPLON** leaps with his pod.

5. Giant **NAMTA** rays can grow to nine metres across.

6. Brightly coloured **CHINWOLFS** have funny name.

7. Beware not to step on a spiny sea **RICHUN**.

8. **ALFHINGERS** are heavenly coloured reef dwellers.

11. Silver **ABRACURDA** have sharp teeth and are good hunters.

13. **LEE** loves to conga or moray.

15. THE big mouthed **ROPERUG** doesn't like to be alone.

16. Squashy **ENGPOS** look at home on the reef or in the bathroom.

17. These **CALM** secretive shellfish can live up to five hundred years.

19. Green and loggerhead **ERLTUT** come to the beach to lay their eggs.

21. **ALEC BRAN** loves rock clinging and waiting for the tide to feed.

23. Sharp-toothed, **HARKS** have a fearsome reputation.

24. If they sold ink they'd be **QUIDS** in.

Answers on page 267.

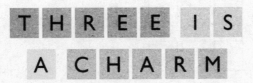

THREE IS A CHARM

Can you rearrange this list of TWENTY SEVEN weirdly random words into NINE entirely not weird three-word phrases? The first has been completed for you.

READY   AGE   AT   WHEEL   SIGHT   IS
LESS   GAP   ~~THREE~~   POSSIBLE   ~~WORD~~   LIFE
GO   FIRST   LARGER   BEAUTY   MIND   SET
DRIVE   FOUR   MORE   IS   ~~PHRASE~~   THE
ANYTHING   BEFORE   THAN

Example:

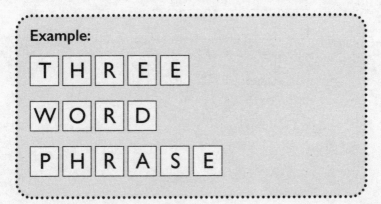

THREE
WORD
PHRASE

1.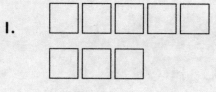

2.
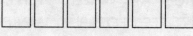

3.

4.

5.

6.

7.

8.

Answers on page 267.

Each of the following statements contains one word that makes it too weird to be true. Can you replace one word in each of sentences to make it make sense?

Example:

The baboon is a woodwind instrument with two reeds which plays bass and tenor notes.

The ~~baboon~~ is a woodwind instrument with two reeds which plays bass and tenor notes.

The **BASSOON** is a woodwind instrument with two reeds which plays bass and tenor notes.

161

FLUTE   SOPRANO   BATON   PIT
~~BASSOON~~   OPERAS   PERCUSSION
COMPOSER   CELLOS

1. A small clarinet is called a piccolo.

☐☐☐☐☐

2. The conductor uses a baguette to conduct
the orchestra.

☐☐☐☐☐

3. The string section has violas, violins, bellows
and double basses.

☐☐☐☐☐☐

4. The pincushion section helps the orchestra keep
to the beat.

☐☐☐☐☐☐☐☐☐☐

5. A singer with a high-pitched voice is called a sourpuss.

☐☐☐☐☐☐☐

6. Ludvig van Beethoven was a famous bulldozer.

☐☐☐☐☐☐☐☐

7. Dramatic performances in which many of the words are sung are called operations or musicals.

☐☐☐☐☐☐

8. In theatrical performances with music musicians play in an area between the audience in stage called the orchestra patch.

☐☐☐

9. The trombone is part of the brass section of the orchestra along with the horn, tuba and crumpet.

☐☐☐☐☐☐☐

Answers on page 267.

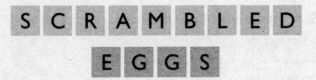

SCRAMBLED EGGS

The breakfast menu board at the Seafront Café is in a bit of a muddle. Can you unscramble the menu items so the beachgoers can have their breakfast?

1. MADDALENA ASTROMAT

| | | | | | | | | |
|---|---|---|---|---|---|---|---|---| £2.50

2. BAFFLING WEASEL

| | | | | | |
|---|---|---|---|---|---| £5.00

164

3. ARTHUR DINGY TOFU

□□□□□□□

□□□ □□□□□ £4.00

4. BAGGED CANONS

□□□□□

□□□ □□□□ £5.00

5. SLUG ALA ROSE

□□□□□□□

□□□□ £1.50

6. WAGGED CHINS

□□□

□□□□□□□□ £3.90

7. RIPER DOG

<!-- 8 empty boxes --> £4.00

8. SEETHE TOMECELE

<!-- 6 empty boxes -->

<!-- 8 empty boxes --> £4.20

9. APE SNACK

<!-- 8 empty boxes --> £5.30

10. JENICA ROUGE

<!-- 6 empty boxes -->

<!-- 5 empty boxes --> £2.10

11. CHESTON FART

☐ ☐ ☐ ☐ ☐ ☐

☐ ☐ ☐ ☐ ☐ £6.00

12. U SLIME

☐ ☐ ☐ ☐ ☐ ☐ £4.00

13. ECOEFF

☐ ☐ ☐ ☐ ☐ ☐ £1.90

14. EAT

☐ ☐ ☐ £1.75

15. MOO HEIST

☐ ☐ ☐ ☐ ☐ ☐ ☐ ☐ £3.70

Answers on page 267.

FILL THE REFRIGERATOR

All of these items belong in the refrigerator. Can you work out where they go using the number of letters in each word?

THREE LETTERS
PIE
HAM
COD

FOUR LETTERS
MILK
TOFU
MEAT

FIVE LETTERS
CREAM
JUICE

SIX LETTERS
CHEESE
BUTTER
CELERY

SEVEN LETTERS
YOGHURT

LETTUCE
AVOCADO
PEPPERS
CARROTS

EIGHT LETTERS
CUCUMBER

NINE LETTERS
LEFTOVERS

TEN LETTERS
MAYONNAISE

ELEVEN LETTERS
BLUEBERRIES

TWELVE LETTERS
STRAWBERRIES

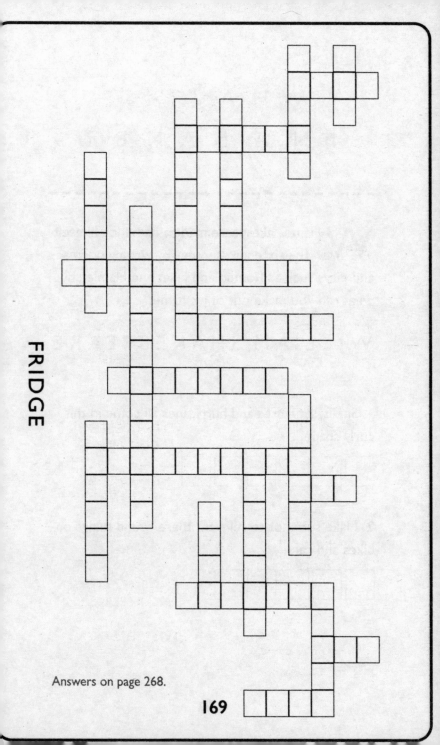

FRIDGE

Answers on page 268.

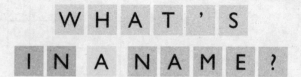

WHAT'S IN A NAME?

William Shakespeare made a name for himself in the sixteenth century by writing poems and plays such as Romeo and Juliet and Hamlet, but what can you make out of his name?

WILLIAM SHAKESPEARE

1. Shells, staircases and hurricanes all come in this curly shape.

☐ ☐ ☐ ☐ ☐ ☐

2. Make sure not to reinvent these round things on bikes and cars.

☐ ☐ ☐ ☐ ☐

3. Stir with this wire thing to make your eggs fluffy.

☐☐☐☐☐

4. Blue, pilot, sperm and beluga are all members of this family of ocean mammals.

☐☐☐☐☐

5. These trees make delicious syrup.

☐☐☐☐☐

6. Small, round vegetable that grows in a pod.

☐☐☐

7. Put one foot in front of the other.

☐☐☐☐

8. Don't forget to say this and thank you, if you want to be polite.

☐☐☐☐☐☐

9. Speak softly into a person's ear.

☐☐☐☐☐☐☐

10. The northernmost state in the United States of America.

☐☐☐☐☐☐

11. Pigs love to eat this.

☐☐☐☐☐

12. A rice dish enjoyed in Spain.

☐☐☐☐☐☐

13. Babies can be pushed along in one of these.

☐☐☐☐

14. A dream, or hope, a genie will grant you three of.

☐☐☐☐

15. Gem found inside an oyster.

☐☐☐☐☐

16. A warm scarf worn around the shoulders.

☐☐☐☐☐

17. Hairy, green, tropical fruit.

☐☐☐☐

18. Diamonds, bubbly water and great personalities do this.

☐☐☐☐☐☐☐

Answers on page 268.

CRYPTIC CATCHPHRASES

Use the cipher to below to complete these common phrases. Can you find which phrase is the odd one out and why?

A	B	C	D	E	F	G	H	I	J	K	L	M
Z	Y	X	W	V	U	T	S	R	Q	P	O	N

N	O	P	Q	R	S	T	U	V	W	X	Y	Z
M	L	K	J	I	H	G	F	E	D	C	B	A

1. KFG BLFI YVHG ULLG ULIDZIW

2. SVZW RM GSV XOLFWH

□ □ □ □ □ □

□ □ □ □ □ □ □ □ □

3. YB GSV HPRM LU BLFI GVVGS

□ □ □ □ □ □ □ □ □ □

□ □ □ □ □ □

□ □ □ □ □

4. ZG GSV WILK LU Z SZG

□ □ □ □ □ □ □ □ □ □

□ □ □ □ □ □

5. TREV GSV XLOW HSLFOWVR

□ □ □ □ □ □ □ □ □ □ □

□ □ □ □ □ □ □ □

6. SRG GSV MZRO LM GSV SVZW

□□□ □□□□ □□□ □□□□

□□ □□□ □□□□ □□□

7. XLHG ZM ZIN ZMW Z OVY

□□□□ □□ □□□ □□□

□□□ □ □□□ □

8. KFOORMT BLFI OVT

□□□□□□□ □□□□

□□□□ □□□ □□□

9. TVG RG LUU BLFI XSVHG

□□□ □□ □□□ □□□□

□□□□□ □□□□□□

10. KFG Z ULLG RM RG

□□□□

□□□□ □□ □□

Answers on pages 268-9.

THREE
LITTLE WORDS

Can you rearrange this list of THIRTY weirdly random words into TEN entirely not weird three-word phrases? The first has been completed for you.

DEAD   PIE   ~~DOTS~~   DO   SINS   JOY
AS   BACK   BURSTING   EDGED   CROSS
BUNDLE   DEADLY   HEART   EASY   PRIDE
DOUBLE   SEVEN   ATTITUDE   ~~JOIN~~
SWORD   CAN   GORGEOUS   YOUR   ~~THE~~
COME   DROP   WITH   OF   SOON

Example:

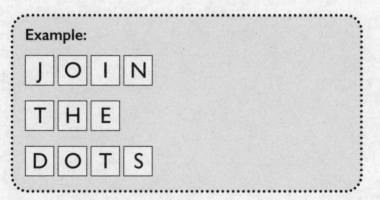

J O I N

T H E

D O T S

178

1.

☐☐☐☐☐☐

☐☐

☐☐☐

2.

☐☐☐☐☐

☐☐☐☐☐☐

☐☐☐☐

3.

☐☐☐☐☐☐☐☐

☐☐☐☐

☐☐☐☐☐

4.

▢▢▢

▢▢

▢▢▢▢▢▢▢▢

5.

▢▢▢▢

▢▢▢▢

▢▢▢▢

6.

▢▢▢▢▢

▢▢▢▢

▢▢▢▢▢

180

7.

□ □ □ □ □ □

□ □ □ □ □

□ □ □ □ □

8.

□ □ □ □

□ □ □ □

□ □ □ □ □ □ □ □

9

□ □ □ □

□ □

□ □ □

Answers on page 269.

Can you solve these wordy riddles?

1. Which eight letter word contains all 26 letters?

☐☐☐☐☐☐☐☐

2. Which six letter word becomes twelve when you take one letter away?

☐☐☐☐☐☐

3. Which three letter word is very heavy forward but is not backwards?

☐☐☐

4. Which word of three letters is fewer when you add two more?

☐☐☐

5. Which solitary three letter word is no less alone when you add two more letters?

▢▢▢

6. Which five letter word reads the same forwards, backwards and upside down?

▢▢▢▢▢

Answers on page 269.

FIND THE JOEY

A kangaroo word is a word that contains a shorter synonym (word with a similar meaning) to itself. This synonym is called a 'joey'. In order to be a true kangaroo word, the letters of the joey have to be in the correct order. Look at the words below and see if you can find the joeys hidden inside.

Example:

KANGAROO

O	B	S	E	R	V	E

O	B	S	E	R	V	E

JOEY

S	E	E

184

1.

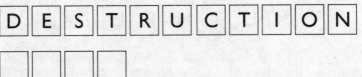

D E S T R U C T I O N

☐ ☐ ☐ ☐

2.

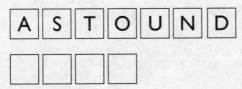

A S T O U N D

☐ ☐ ☐ ☐

3.

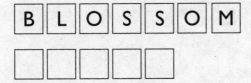

B L O S S O M

☐ ☐ ☐ ☐ ☐

4.

R A M P A G E

☐ ☐ ☐ ☐

5.

| T | R | U | T | H | F | U | L | L | Y |

| | | | | |

6.

| S | T | E | A | L | T | H | Y |

| | | |

7.

| C | A | V | E | R | N |

| | | | |

8.

| L | A | T | E | S | T |

| | | | |

9.

I L L U M I N A T E D

☐ ☐ ☐

10.

H O N O U R A B L E

☐ ☐ ☐ ☐ ☐

Answers on page 269.

HIP OR HOP

All of these words or phrases contain the words **HIP** or **HOP** or both. Use the clues to help you discover which words they are.

Example:

Striped rodent famous for singing and eating nuts.

1. Lamb, pork or karate.

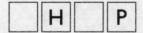

2. A wish that a person can hold on to long term.

3. A game which involves jumping on one leg between squares.

H		P						

4. Buy battered fish and fried potato sticks here.

	H		P		H		P

5. Slang term for an enormous lie.

	H		P			

6. Chess piece which can only move diagonally on the board.

			H		P

7. Use a whisk to do this to cream or egg whites.

	H		P

8. Sail across the ocean in one of these.

	H		P

9. Large mammal often found in and around watering holes in southern Africa.

H		P		

10. Robinson Crusoe was stranded on a desert island after one of these.

	H		P					

11. Pair of joints at the top of the legs. Wiggle them when you dance.

H		P	

Answers on page 269.

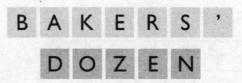

Baker's assistant, Ciara Currantbun's computer keyboard was involved in a horrific jam accident leaving all of the vowel keys very sticky. Can you work out what the baker needs to bake this week from her list?

A E I O U

Example:

CHCLT CLRS

C	H	O	C	O	L	A	T	E

E	C	L	A	I	R	S

1. CSTRD SLCS

⬜⬜⬜⬜⬜⬜⬜

⬜⬜⬜⬜⬜⬜

2. ICD BNS

⬜⬜⬜⬜ ⬜⬜⬜⬜

3. SSGE RLLS

⬜⬜⬜⬜⬜⬜⬜

⬜⬜⬜⬜⬜

4. DNSH PSTRS

⬜⬜⬜⬜⬜⬜

⬜⬜⬜⬜⬜⬜⬜⬜

192

5. JM DGHNTS

☐☐☐

☐☐☐☐☐☐☐☐☐

6. CHCLT CHP CKS

☐☐☐☐☐☐☐☐☐

☐☐☐☐

☐☐☐☐☐☐☐

7. SCNS

☐☐☐☐☐☐

8. PPL TRNVRS

☐☐☐☐☐

☐☐☐☐☐☐☐☐☐

9. BLBRRY MFFNS

☐☐☐☐☐☐☐☐☐

☐☐☐☐☐☐☐

10. BNN LVS

☐☐☐☐☐☐

☐☐☐☐☐☐

11. CRNSH PSTS

☐☐☐☐☐☐☐

☐☐☐☐☐☐☐☐

12. BKWLL TRTS

☐☐☐☐☐☐☐☐☐

☐☐☐☐☐

Answers on page 270.

MONUMENTAL ERRORS

Kiran the careless travel influencer forgot to run a spellcheck before publishing his latest blog. Can you unscramble the famous monuments and landmarks Kiran visited this month?

Example:

I enjoyed a croissant in Paris beneath the **ELFIE TWOFER**.

E	I	F	F	E	L

T	O	W	E	R

1. In Rome, I cycled all the way around the ancient and poetic **COSMO LUES**.

2. In New York, I rode in a helicopter around the towering green **BEAST FURY TOILET**

3. In London, I saw **ANGELICA HUMPBACK** and watched the changing of the guard.

4. In Salisbury I saw an ancient rocky circle people call **GENE HESTON**.

5. In Agra, India I wondered at the ivory-white **JAMAL HAT**.

6. While in Scotland's capital city I climbed Arthur's seat and visited **CHRISTABEL NUDGE**.

[ ][ ][ ][ ][ ][ ][ ][ ][ ]

[ ][ ][ ][ ][ ][ ]

7. In Belfast, I watched the waves crash over the majestic **ANGUS CAYEWAIST**.

[ ][ ][ ][ ][ ]['][ ]

[ ][ ][ ][ ][ ][ ][ ][ ]

8. In Egypt, I saw the largest tomb, that of the Pharaoh Khufu the **GAMAYFIRG TRAPEZOID**.

[ ][ ][ ][ ][ ]

[ ][ ][ ][ ][ ][ ][ ]

[ ][ ] [ ][ ][ ][ ]

Answers on page 270.

BIG TOP
WEIRD SEARCH

Can you find all twenty circus words in the grid? It's a tricky one. Words can be arranged in any direction: backwards, forwards as well as diagonal.

E	E	A	I	F	H	Y	A	Q	S	X	T	P	P	X
C	L	C	W	N	I	F	W	S	W	N	T	N	D	S
I	C	R	K	E	Q	R	O	C	L	O	W	N	T	L
F	Y	O	T	T	M	L	E	S	P	P	N	R	G	W
F	C	B	V	O	F	U	E	E	X	Z	O	O	J	O
O	I	A	X	Y	P	S	T	J	A	N	Z	T	U	R
X	N	T	D	R	R	H	E	S	G	T	R	N	G	N
O	U	N	F	O	C	X	A	M	O	A	E	C	G	R
B	A	Z	H	K	S	X	A	T	P	C	B	R	L	O
C	A	U	D	I	E	N	C	E	N	W	I	T	E	C
K	N	L	Y	R	E	T	S	A	M	G	N	I	R	P
D	E	P	L	A	T	E	S	P	I	N	N	E	R	O
A	G	X	C	O	N	A	I	C	I	G	A	M	Y	P
I	F	I	E	P	O	R	T	H	G	I	T	Y	D	G
E	F	V	O	L	E	N	I	L	O	P	M	A	R	T

CLOWN

BALLOON

ACROBAT

STRONG MAN

RING MASTER

COSTUME

POPCORN

CANDYFLOSS

AUDIENCE

FIREEATER

JUGGLER

MAGICIAN

SWORD SWALLOWER

PLATE SPINNER

TIGHTROPE

BOX OFFICE

TRAMPOLINE

UNICYCLE

HORSES

TOP HAT

Answers on page 270.

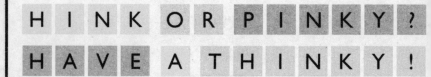

HINKORPINKY?
HAVEATHINKY!

A hink pink is a rhyming pair of ONE SYLLABLE words that answer a question. A hinky pinky is a rhyming pair of TWO SYLLABLE words that answer a question. Can you work out the hink pinks AND hinky pinkies that answer these silly questions?

Example.

What do you call green dirt?

LIME GRIME

What do you call foolish man named William?

SILLY BILLY

200

1. What do you call an enormous container of plant-based, butter-like spread?

☐ ☐ ☐ ☐ ☐ ☐ ☐ ☐ ☐ ☐

2. What do you call a savoury tart that will appeal to a limited audience?

☐ ☐ ☐ ☐ ☐ ☐ ☐ ☐ ☐ ☐

3. What do you call a box you keep an orthodontic appliance in?

☐ ☐ ☐ ☐ ☐ ☐ ☐ ☐ ☐

4. What do you call a big cat made of ferrous metal?

☐ ☐ ☐ ☐ ☐ ☐ ☐ ☐

5. What do you call a person named Elizabeth with too much to do?

☐ ☐ ☐ ☐ ☐ ☐ ☐ ☐ ☐

6. What do you call the wettest person in a rain-soaked tent?

☐ ☐ ☐ ☐ ☐ ☐

☐ ☐ ☐ ☐ ☐ ☐

7. What do you call a nit living on a small rodent?

☐ ☐ ☐ ☐ ☐ ☐ ☐ ☐ ☐ ☐

8. What do you call a waft of brie?

☐ ☐ ☐ ☐ ☐

☐ ☐ ☐ ☐ ☐

9. What do you call a long story that takes place in a farm building?

☐ ☐ ☐ ☐ ☐ ☐ ☐ ☐

10. What do you call the instrument you use for tracing outlines?

☐ ☐ ☐ ☐ ☐

☐ ☐ ☐ ☐ ☐

11. What do you call gravy or custard that is filled with lumps?

☐ ☐ ☐ ☐ ☐ ☐ ☐ ☐ ☐ ☐ ☐

12. What do you call a photograph taken at Santa's Grotto?

☐ ☐ ☐ ☐ ☐ ☐ ☐ ☐ ☐ ☐ ☐

13. What do you call a torn gift voucher?

☐ ☐ ☐ ☐ ☐ ☐ ☐ ☐ ☐ ☐ ☐

14. What do you call a sweet dropped on the beach?

☐ ☐ ☐ ☐ ☐ ☐ ☐ ☐ ☐ ☐

15. What do you call a pompom shaped like a turkey?

☐ ☐ ☐ ☐ ☐ ☐

☐ ☐ ☐ ☐ ☐ ☐

Answers on page 270.

THREE IS A MAGIC NUMBER

Can you rearrange this list of THIRTY weirdly random words into TEN entirely not weird three-word phrases? The first has been completed for you.

AWAY   DANDY   FORGET   ~~JACKPOT~~   SWIM
GOLD   HEART   CARE   COIN   AND   OR
~~THE~~   CARRIED   A   ~~HIT~~   MATCH   HANDLE
SET   BROKE   FORGIVE   GAME   SINK   FINE
GOING   AND   FOR   WITH   OF   GET   FLIP

Example.

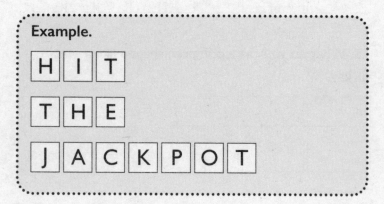

H I T

T H E

J A C K P O T

1. □ □ □ □

□ □

□ □ □ □

2. □ □ □ □

□

□ □ □ □

3. □ □ □ □

□ □ □

□ □ □ □ □

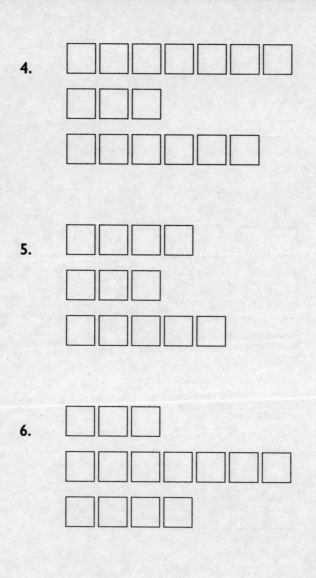

7.

☐☐☐☐☐

☐☐☐

☐☐☐☐☐

8.

☐☐☐☐☐☐

☐☐☐☐

☐☐☐☐

9.

☐☐☐☐☐

☐☐

☐☐☐☐

Answers on page 271.

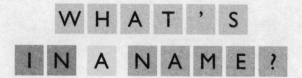

WHAT'S IN A NAME?

Simone Biles made a name for herself by winning more gold medals in international competition than any other gymnast, but what can you make out of her name?

SIMONE BILES

1. Run twenty six of these to complete a marathon.

☐ ☐ ☐ ☐ ☐

2. Female, African big cat.

☐ ☐ ☐ ☐ ☐ ☐ ☐

3. Long car, often found transporting celebrities.

☐ ☐ ☐ ☐

4. Hung over a crib to keep a baby entertained.

☐ ☐ ☐ ☐ ☐ ☐

5. Sour, yellow citrus.

☐ ☐ ☐ ☐ ☐

6. A place to dig up things that aren't yours.

☐ ☐ ☐ ☐

7. A snooty person.

☐ ☐ ☐ ☐

8. An arch enemy.

☐ ☐ ☐ ☐ ☐ ☐ ☐

9. An important task which may involve travel.

☐ ☐ ☐ ☐ ☐ ☐ ☐

10. Ancient king of Crete with a labyrinth in his basement.

☐☐☐☐☐

11. A game in which only this guy can tell players what to do.

☐☐☐☐☐

12. Nickname of Scotland's most famous mythical monster.

☐☐☐☐☐☐

13. A self-propelled weapon capable of travelling long distances.

☐☐☐☐☐☐☐

14. A male child.

☐☐☐

15. Famous A.A. who wrote Winnie the Pooh.

☐☐☐☐☐

16. Formal and sincere, certainly not jolly.

☐☐☐☐☐☐

Answers on page 271.

GORDON
HAVE MORSEY!

-- --

Neelay and Tim live across the road from one another. They like to play at being detectives. After they go to bed, Neelay and Tim use torches to flash messages to one another across the street in Morse code. A short flash means a dot and a long flash is a dash.

Their latest case is discovering who is making holes in Neelay's garden. Neelay's father blames the squirrels while Neelay's mother think that Neelay and Tim made them in a game and won't let them play in the garden until they have filled them up. Tim thinks he knows what is going on.

MORSE CODE

A	B	C	D	E	F	G	H	I	J	K	L	M
•-	-•••	-•-•	-••	•	••-•	--•	••••	••	•---	-•-	•-••	--

N	O	P	Q	R	S	T	U	V	W	X	Y	Z
-•	---	•--•	--•-	•-•	•••	-	••-	•••-	•--	-••-	-•--	--••

Decode the following messages and answer the
questions.

-- •-• / •--• •- •-•• -- • •-• / ••-• •-• --- --/ -• • -••- - -•• --- --- •-•/

....

•-•• • -/ •••• •• •••/ -•• --- --•/ --• --- •-• -•• --- --•/ •• -•

....

/ -•-- --- ••- •-• / --• •- •-• -•• • -•/

....

--• --- •-• -•• --- --•/ •• ••• / -•• •• --• --• •• -• --•/

....

- •- -•- •/ •-/ •--• •• -•-• - ••- •-• •/

....

••• •••• --- •-- / -•-- --- ••- •-• / -- ••-

....

1. Who is making the holes in the garden?
2. Who let him in?
3. Where do they live?
4. How will they prove it?

Answers on page 271.

213

WORD LADDER

Follow the clues and change one letter at a time to create a brand new word.

S I N G

A male monarch.

☐ ☐ ☐ ☐

Friendly type.

☐ ☐ ☐ ☐

The best thing to do with your own business.

☐ ☐ ☐ ☐

Not yours or theirs.

☐ ☐ ☐ ☐

A lion's coiffure.

☐ ☐ ☐ ☐

Often found winding in the country, motorways have many.

☐ ☐ ☐ ☐

Unable to walk.

☐ ☐ ☐ ☐

A friendly beast.

☐ ☐ ☐ ☐

A precious thing to tell.

☐ ☐ ☐ ☐

To act without words.

☐ ☐ ☐ ☐

Mickey and Minnie are...

Roll to play.

D I C E

Answers on page 271.

216

- -

Follow the clues and fill in the missing letters to solve the puzzle. None of the letters that are crossed out appear in the words. The greyed out letters have been placed for you.

1. Find the best of them at CRUFTS.

A B ~~C~~ D E F G H ~~I~~ ~~J~~ K L M
N O P ~~Q~~ R ~~S~~ ~~T~~ U ~~V~~ ~~W~~ ~~X~~ ~~Y~~ ~~Z~~

B		L	L	D	O		

	O	O	D	L	

L		B			D	O	

B	L	O	O	D		O			D

They are all types of: | D | O | |

217

2. Their wings may 'bug' you.

A B C D E F G̶ H I J K̶ L M̶
N̶ O̶ P̶ Q̶ R S T U V̶ W̶ X Y Z̶

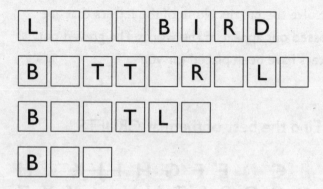

| L | | | | B | I | R | D |

| B | | T | T | | R | | L | |

| B | | | T | L | |

| B | | |

They are all types of:
| I | | | | | | T |

3. Though they may slither, they are smooth and not slimy.

A B C D̶ E F̶ G̶ H I J K L M̶
N O P Q̶ R S T U̶ V̶ W̶ X̶ Y Z̶

| P | | T | | | O | N |

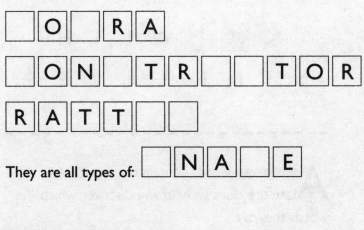

| | O | | R | A |

| | O | N | | T | R | | | T | O | R |

| R | A | T | T | | |

They are all types of: | | N | A | | E |

4. 'Finned' them in ocean.

A B C D E F G H I J K L M
N O P Q R S T U V W X Y Z

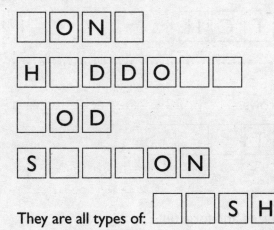

| | O | N | |

| H | | D | D | O | | |

| | O | D |

| S | | | O | N |

They are all types of: | | | S | H |

Answers on page 272.

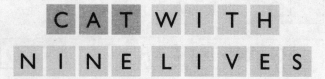

CAT WITH NINE LIVES

All of these words contain the word **CAT**. Use the clues to help you discover which words they are.

> **Example:**
>
> Use both hands to grab the ball from the air.
>
> | C | A | T | C | H |
> |---|---|---|---|---|

1. Lots of cows.

C	A	T			

2. Disorganized and forgetful.

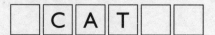

	C	A	T		

3. Fragile.

| | | | | C | A | T | |

4. Very detailed.

| | | | | | C | A | T | |

5. To provide food for an event.

| C | A | T | | |

6. Place.

| | | C | A | T | | | |

7. A full-length leotard.

| C | A | T | | | | |

8. A large church in a city.

| C | A | T | | | | | |

Answers on page 272.

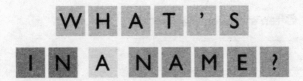

WHAT'S IN A NAME?

- -

Greta Thunberg made a name for herself with her activism and campaigning on behalf of the environment, but what can you make out of her name.

GRETA THUNBERG

1. To come back.

☐☐☐☐☐☐

2. Its beat is at the centre of things.

☐☐☐☐☐

3. Something to aim for.

☐☐☐☐☐☐

4. Often stranger than fiction.

☐☐☐☐☐

5. A small, useful boat.

☐☐☐

6. Everyone needs this embrace.

☐☐☐

7. A red gemstone.

☐☐☐☐☐☐

8. Older than twelve but younger than twenty.

☐☐☐☐

9. Often made of chicken, vegetables or gold.

☐☐☐☐☐☐

10. When the need is desperate.

☐☐☐☐☐☐

11. Ancient king with a liking for round tables.

☐☐☐☐☐☐

12. To remove something's innards.

☐☐☐

13. Another word for a spy. Secret...

☐☐☐☐☐

14. Despite their name, these meat/vegetable sandwiches are rarely, if ever, made of ham.

☐☐☐☐☐☐☐

15. Dairy-based, yellow spread.

☐☐☐☐☐☐

Answers on page 272.

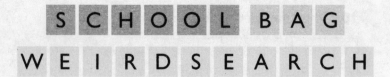

SCHOOL BAG
WEIRDSEARCH

Can you find all twenty back-to-school items in the grid? Some items are harder to find than others.

V	G	L	Y	V	S	C	I	S	S	O	R	S	T	K
H	M	L	L	U	N	C	H	B	O	X	O	D	E	P
O	P	P	U	K	F	O	L	D	E	R	R	R	X	E
M	V	R	H	E	C	E	X	L	Z	P	X	I	T	N
E	H	W	O	I	S	R	O	T	X	E	Z	N	B	C
W	N	S	C	T	G	T	A	A	H	N	G	K	O	I
O	O	S	T	A	R	H	I	Y	S	S	V	S	O	L
R	T	H	R	I	L	A	L	C	O	E	O	B	K	C
K	E	A	P	R	C	C	C	I	K	N	R	O	W	A
R	B	R	E	U	P	K	U	T	G	B	S	T	H	S
Y	O	P	N	L	E	R	Y	L	O	H	J	T	O	E
C	O	E	C	E	K	I	Q	T	A	R	T	L	I	C
U	K	N	I	R	I	U	V	T	A	T	D	E	O	S
S	H	E	L	D	T	F	L	C	A	P	O	W	R	N
D	M	R	S	R	U	B	B	E	R	W	E	R	N	V

NOTEBOOK

PENCILS

PENS

SCISSORS

GLUESTICK

STICKY TAPE

TEXTBOOK

RUBBER

RULER

SHARPENER

CRAYONS

CALCULATOR

PROTRACTOR

FOLDER

DRINKS BOTTLE

LUNCH BOX

PENCILCASE

PE KIT

HIGHLIGHTER

HOMEWORK

Answers on page 272.

BOX WORDS

This grid contains six animals. The first letter of each animal can be found in column one, the second in column two etc. Can you find all six of the concealed creatures?

1 2 3 4 5 6

1	2	3	4	5	6
M	I	A	U	A	R
J	O	U	V	E	Y
B	E	N	G	O	N
C	A	B	K	E	Y
D	O	N	P	A	R
G	O	G	K	E	R

M □ □ □ □ □

J □ □ □ □ □

B □ □ □ □ □

228

Answers on page 273.

B U T   I N

All of these words have the word **BUT** in them. Use the clues to help you fill in the words.

Example:

Without a zip, fasten your clothes with these.

| B | U | T | T | O | N | S |

---

1. Another word for a navel.

2. A person who specializes in preparing meat.

3. Pear-shaped squash, delicious in soup.

4. Large, flat fish found in the ocean.

| | | | | B | U | T |

5. Island in the Firth of Clyde, Scotland.

| B | U | T | |

6. A manservant in a large house.

| B | U | T | | | |

7. Plant with yellow flowers found in fields and hedgerows.

| B | U | T | | | | | | |

8. A sandwich filled with chips.

| B | U | T | | |

9. Bottoms have two of these.

| B | U | T | | | | |

10. Made of brick or stone, they provide support to buildings.

| B | U | T | | | | | |

11. A caterpillar's final destination.

| B | U | T | | | | | | |

12. To make a first appearance.

| | | B | U | T |

13. To give something.

| | | | | | | B | U | T | |

14. A person who drops things all the time.

| B | U | T | | | |

| | | | | | |

Answers on page 273.

MIXED-UP SUBJECTS

Believe it or not, all of the weird words below are mixed-up school subjects. Can you unscramble them to become top of the class?

1. AGGRO HYPE

☐☐☐☐☐☐☐☐

2. SHIRT YO

☐☐☐☐☐☐☐

3. ATTACH MIMES

☐☐☐☐☐☐☐☐☐☐☐

4. SHIN GEL

☐☐☐☐☐☐☐

233

5. CINE SEC

6. CHEF RN

7. HI SNAPS

8. ANTS DREADING

9. I SCUM

10. GOT MIC PUN

Answers on page 273.

In the 1800s Florence Nightingale made a name for herself as a skilled nurse and by using her knowledge of maths to help reform the care of sick and injured people. What can you make out of her name?

FLORENCE NIGHTINGALE

1. Game played on a course with balls and clubs.

☐☐☐☐

2. To disagree, sometimes with fists.

☐☐☐☐☐

3. To provide with something to wear.

☐☐☐☐☐☐

4. A country that is not your own.

☐☐☐☐☐☐☐

5. Towers. Theme park in Stoke-on-Trent, England.

☐☐☐☐☐

6. Horned mammal that can be found in Southern Africa.

☐☐☐☐☐

7. Dessert made from jelly and custard.

☐☐☐☐☐☐

8. A chair fit for a queen.

☐☐☐☐☐☐

9. A dog's favourite game.

☐☐☐☐☐

10. Gas which makes up more than 70% of the Earth's atmosphere.

☐☐☐☐☐☐☐☐

11. A musical about a girl with red hair and no parents.

☐☐☐☐☐

12. Evergreen trees that produce cones.

☐☐☐☐☐☐☐

13. What someone does when they are embarrassed.

☐☐☐☐☐☐

14. The son of Prince Harry.

□□□□□□

15. Scottish lake.

□□□□

Answers on page 273.

MISSING TYPE

---

ollow the clues and fill in the missing letters to solve the puzzle. None of the letters that are crossed out appear in the words. The greyed out letters have been placed for you.

1. Polished, cut and set these fetch a fine price.

A B ~~C~~ D E ~~F~~ ~~G~~ H I J ~~K~~ L M
~~N~~ ~~O~~ P Q R S ~~T~~ U ~~V~~ W ~~X~~ Y ~~Z~~

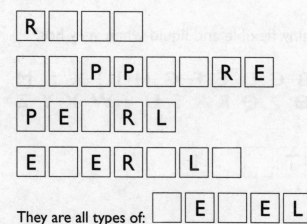

R			

		P	P			R	E

P	E		R	L

E		E	R	L	

They are all types of:

	E		E	L

239

2. Perfect for drawing, folding and recycling.

A B̶ ̶C̶ ̶D E F̶ G H I J̶ ̶K̶ ̶L̶ M
N O̶ P Q̶ R S T U V̶ W X̶ ̶Y̶ ̶Z̶

W			P	P	I		G

W		I		I		G

	I	S	S		E

D			W	I		G

They are all types of :

P		P	E	

3. Shiny, flexible and liquid when very hot.

A B̶ C̶ D E F̶ ̶G̶ H I J̶ ̶K̶ L M
N O̶ P Q̶ R S T U̶ V W̶ ̶X̶ ̶Y̶ ̶Z̶

S	T			L

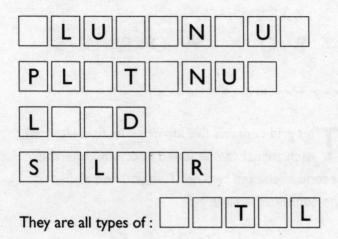

| | L | U | | | N | | U | |

| P | L | | T | | | N | U | |

| L | | | D |

| S | | L | | | R |

They are all types of : | | | T | | L |

BOX WORDS

This grid contains five animals. The first letter of each animal can be found in column one, the second in column two etc. Can you find all five of the concealed creatures?

	1	2	3	4	5
	C	I	B	L	A
	K	A	G	E	R
	E	O	A	R	E
	T	E	G	L	A
	Z	A	M	E	L

C				

K				

E				

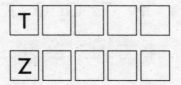

Answers on page 274.

CRYPTOGRAM CONCERTOS

- -

Use the cipher to below to complete these common phrases. Can you find which phrase is the odd one out and why?

A	B	C	D	E	F	G	H	I	J	K	L	M
Z	Y	X	W	V	U	T	S	R	Q	P	O	N

N	O	P	Q	R	S	T	U	V	W	X	Y	Z
M	L	K	J	I	H	G	F	E	D	C	B	A

I. YOLD BLFI LDM GIFNKVG

244

2. KOZBRMT HVXLMV URWWOV

⬜⬜⬜⬜⬜⬜⬜

⬜⬜⬜⬜⬜⬜

⬜⬜⬜⬜⬜⬜

3. NZIXS GL GSV YVZG LU BLFI LDM WIFN

⬜⬜⬜⬜⬜ ⬜⬜ ⬜⬜⬜ ⬜

⬜⬜⬜⬜ ⬜⬜ ⬜⬜⬜⬜

⬜⬜⬜⬜ ⬜⬜⬜⬜

4. YIVZP Z OVT

⬜⬜⬜⬜⬜ ⬜ ⬜⬜⬜

5. KIVZXS GL GSW XSLRI

⬜⬜⬜⬜⬜⬜ ⬜⬜ ⬜⬜⬜⬜

⬜⬜⬜⬜

245

6. ZOO YVOOH ZMW DSRHGOVH

☐☐☐ ☐☐☐☐☐

☐☐☐ ☐☐☐☐☐☐☐☐

7. UZXV GSV NFHRX

☐☐☐☐ ☐☐☐

☐☐☐☐☐

8. KFNK FK GSV QZN

☐☐☐☐ ☐☐

☐☐☐ ☐☐☐

9. RG GZPVH GDL GL GZMTL

☐☐ ☐☐☐☐☐ ☐☐☐

☐☐ ☐☐☐☐☐

10. XSZMTV BLFI GFMV

☐☐☐☐☐☐ ☐☐☐☐

☐☐☐☐

11. WZMXV ORPV MLYLWB RH
DZGXSRMT

☐☐☐☐☐ ☐☐☐☐

☐☐☐☐☐☐ ☐☐

☐☐☐☐☐☐☐☐

Answers on page 274.

CAR BOX WORDS

E ach of these grids contains things you find on a car. The first letter of each item can be found in column one, the second in column two etc. Can you find all of the hidden car parts?

	1	2	3	4
	H	X	L	T
	A	O	R	N
	B	Y	R	E
	T	O	O	E

	1	2	3	4	5
	R	H	G	H	S
	W	A	A	R	T
	B	I	D	E	O
	G	R	E	K	L
	L	E	A	I	E

BODY PARTS

A ll of the body parts below fit in the grid. Can you work out where they go by using counting the squares and using the number of letters in each word?

THREE LETTERS
EAR
HIP
LIP
EYE
TOE

FOUR LETTERS
BACK
CALF
NOSE
NECK
KNEE
HEAD
SKIN
FOOT
VEIN

FIVE LETTERS
BRAIN
LUNGS
LIVER
MOUTH
ANKLE
ELBOW

THIGH
HEART
CHEST

SIX LETTERS
SPLEEN
FINGER
TONGUE
KIDNEY
MUSCLE
NERVES

SEVEN LETTERS
STOMACH
KNUCKLE

EIGHT LETTERS
SKELETON
SHOULDER

NINE LETTERS
INTESTINE

Answers on page 275.

BONUS HINKETY PINKETIES

A hinkety pinkety is a rhyming pair of THREE SYLLABLE words that answer a question. Can you work out the hinkety pinketies that answer these silly questions?

1. What do you call a conversation about drums and xylophones?

2. What is another name for the White House in the United States?

252

3. What do you call a raffle in which you can with cups and vases?

4. What do you call a hoofed mammal constructed from orange melons?

5. What do you call a detective story sent in the past?

6. What do you call a stage made of salt?

7. What do you call a Christmas play set at sea?

□ □ □ □ □ □ □ □

□ □ □ □ □ □ □ □ □

8. What do you call a shop that sells forged pastries?

□ □ □ □ □ □

□ □ □ □ □ □

Answers on page 275.

A N S W E R S

Beside the Seaside
1. STICK OF ROCK
2. BEACH
3. PUNCH AND JUDY
4. FAIRGROUND RIDES
5. ICE CREAM
6. ICE LOLLY
7. PEBBLE
8. ROCKPOOL
9. BEACH HUT
10. SOUVENIR
11. SEASHELL
12. OCEAN
13. WAVE
14. BUCKET AND SPADE
15. GREAT WHITE SHARK
16. SUNSHINE
17. STARFISH
18. SUNCREAM
19. TOWEL

Make It Make Sense
1. LOTION/MOTION
2. SWEETNER/SUGAR
3. LOUGHBOROUGH/LONDON
4. BEING/TURNING
5. SLIME/GRIME
6. JENKINS/HOWARD
7. BAKING/SINGING
8. MOON/STARR
9. BELLS/LADIES
10. FLIES/RINGS

Birds in the Bush
1. OWL
2. FINCH
3. ROBIN
4. HAWK
5. RAVEN
6. KINGFISHER
7. OSTRICH
8. SEAGULL
9. HEN
10. MYNA
11. PIGEONS
12. CRANE

Word Ladder

TRAP
TRIP
GRIP
GRIN
GRAN
GRAM
CRAM
CRAB
DRAB
DRAG
BRAG

Pin Drop

1. SPINE
2. PINK
3. PINT.
4. PINCERS
5. LIMPING
6. PIÑATA
7. PINEAPPLE
8. PORCUPINE
9. SPIN
10. OPINION
11. PINCH
12. TERRAPIN
13. PINKY
14. SPINDLE

Written in the Clouds

1. ALICE IN WONDERLAND
2. CHARLIE AND THE CHOCOLATE FACTORY
3. CHARLOTTE'S WEB
4. HARRY POTTER AND THE PHILOSOPHER'S STONE
5. THE VERY HUNGRY CATERPILLAR

A Mix Up at the Airport

1. AIRPORT SECURITY
2. PASSPORT CONTROL
3. CHECK IN DESK
4. DEPARTURES
5. ARRIVALS
6. PASSENGER
7. AIRLINE PILOT
8. FLIGHT ATTENDANT
9. SUITCASE
10. RUNWAY
11. LOST LUGGAGE
12. DUTY FREE

Games Grid

O	K	E	D	F	X	S	O	P	Q
D	N	T	I	O	A	C	T	N	R
U	J	A	V	O	I	I	E	S	O
J	K	R	I	T	G	T	K	I	U
Y	Z	A	N	B	B	S	C	N	N
Z	E	K	G	A	M	A	I	N	D
K	N	K	L	L	Q	N	R	E	E
N	N	L	C	L	O	M	C	T	R
G	Z	X	I	O	X	Y	M	C	S
R	U	G	B	Y	H	G	F	H	E

Mythical Beast Quest

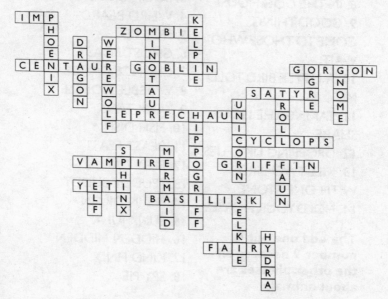

Cryptogram Creatures

1. FISH OUT OF WATER
2. SNUG AS A BUG IN A RUG
3. THE BOY WHO CRIED WOLF
4. STRAIGHT FROM THE HORSE'S MOUTH
5. ON A WILD GOOSE CHASE
6. LET THE CAT OUT OF THE BAG
7. GRAB THE BULL BY THE HORNS
8. IN THE DOG HOUSE
9. GOOD THINGS COME TO THOSE WHO WAIT
10. A LITTLE BIRD TOLD ME
11. TAKING THE LIONS SHARE
12. DROPPING LIKE FLIES
13. KILL TWO BIRDS WITH ONE STONE
14. HOLD YOUR HORSES

The odd one out is number 9 because all the other phrases are about animals.

Happy Heterograms

WALKING
FAMILY
CRUISE
TROPICAL
CAMPING
BEACH

They are all types of HOLIDAY.

Hink Pinks

1. TIME RHYME
2. FUNNY BUNNY
3. BOOK CROOK
4. WEIRD BEARD
5. FREE TEA
6. GHOST ROAST
7. CHANCE DANCE
8. WOBBLE GOBBLE
9. YANK TANK
10. FISH DISH
11. BEAST FEAST
12. PLAY DAY
13. SPUDDY BUDDY
14. PLAIN DRAIN
15. SUNK JUNK
16. HIDDEN MIDDEN
17. KIND FIND
18. SPY PIE

19. LAZY DAISY
20. PROFESSOR DRESSER
21. CHEAP HEAP

Dare You Diltoid?

1. 52 CARDS IN A DECK
2. 11 PLAYERS IN FOOTBALL TEAM
3. 9 LIVES OF A CAT
4. 13 ROLLS IN A BAKER'S DOZEN
5. 2 SHOES IN A PAIR
6. 7 CONTINENTS IN THE WORLD
7. 366 DAYS IN A LEAP YEAR
8. 12 SIGNS OF THE ZODIAC
9. 24 HOURS IN A DAY
10. 8 PLANETS IN THE SOLAR SYSTEM
11. 100 PENNIES IN A POUND
12. 7 COLOURS IN A RAINBOW
13. 26 LETTERS IN THE ALPHABET
14. 288 PAGES IN THIS BOOK

God One Out

1. ZEUS
2. POSEIDON
3. ARTEMIS
4. HERA
5. APHRODITE
6. DIONYSUS
7. THOR
8. HERMES
9. HEPHAESTUS
10. ATHENA
11. ARES
12. APOLLO

Thor is the odd one out because he is a Norse God and not Greek.

Riddle Words

1. SMILES because there is a mile between the first and last letter
2. INVISIBILITY
3. They are in the middle of the OCEAN
4. EGG
5. WORD
6. A DICTIONARY

Qwerty Swap!
1. **FERHAT:** SALMON SUSHI, APPLE JUICE
2. **ELSA:** TURKEY WRAP, FRUIT SALAD
3. **KAI:** TUNA AND CUCUMBER SANDWICH, LEMONADE
4. **ANNA:** ALPHABETTI SPAGHETTI, SILLY SMOOTHIE

What's in a Name?
1. HOOK
2. DONKEY
3. SLEIGH
4. KIOSK
5. KEYHOLE
6. HELEN
7. LEGO
8. ENDING
9. EYELID
10. SILK
11. KIDNEY
12. HONEY
13. KENNEDY
14. YOLK
15. KNEED
16. LEGEND
17. HONKING

Small Change
1. SWORD
2. SORE
3. HISTORY
4. FINAL
5. CON
6. WEST
7. STEAM
8. WIND
9. TWINS
10. SPILL

Hidden Horrors
1. TROLL
2. PHANTOM
3. GHOSTS
4. HAUNT
5. TREAT
6. REAPER
7. TOMB
8. CASKET
9. WAND
10. DEMON
11. HAG
12. CRYPT

The Bin Within
1. CABIN
2. BOBBIN
3. BINGE

4. TURBINE
5. CABINET
6. BINOCULARS
7. TUBING
8. BINDER
9. ROBIN

What's in a Name?
1. DURHAM
2. ORCHARD
3. CHORUS
4. CURDS
5. FARM
6. COD
7. CORFU
8. SMURFS
9. HUM
10. SHARD
11. FORUM
12. MARSH
13. RADAR
14. SURF
15. FOUR
16. CHASM
17. DRAMA
18. HARRODS

Seeing the Wood for the Trees

Out of This World
1. MILKY WAY
2. SATURN
3. BLACK HOLE
4. ANDROMEDA
5. SPACE STATION

Word Ladder
BIKE
LIKE
LIME
MIME
TIME
TAME
TAPE
CAPE

What's in a Name?
1. STRAY
2. TRY
3. TYRES
4. REST
5. TSAR
6. SALTY
7. SET
8. LASHES
9. STAR
10. RASH
11. TESLA
12. RARE
13. SLY
14. HERS
15. RHYS

Fruit Box Words
MELON
PEACH
APPLE
GRAPE
LEMON

The Runed Birthday Party!
Where: THE CASTLE RUINS
What: PIZZA PICNIC
When: 1 p.m. SATURDAY
Bring: VIKING HELMET

A Cat Among the Weirdles
1. INDICATOR
2. SCATTER
3. CATNAP
4. EDUCATE
5. CATALOGUE
6. LOCATION
7. CATCHPHRASE
8. CATAPULT
9. VACATION

Hinky Pinkies
1. CURDLE HURDLE
2. DOG JOG
3. FILE PILE
4. BIGGER DIGGER
5. LARGE BARGE
6. GOAT float
7. FINE BRINE
8. BROWN CROWN
9. MUSTARD CUSTARD
10. WEAKER SEEKER
11. FOUND POUND
12. SCOTCH WATCH
13. SMITTEN KITTEN
14. SORRY LORRY
15. LEAF THIEF

A Bouquet of Vowels

1. DAISY
2. LILY
3. CARNATION
4. IRIS
5. TULIP
6. ANEMONE
7. POPPY
8. PEONY
9. DANDELION
10. VIOLET
11. DAFFODIL

Crossword Contrary

A Mix Up at Lost Property

1. BOBBLE HAT
2. DUFFLE COAT
3. RAILCARD
4. RAINCOAT
5. BASEBALL CAP
6. UMBRELLA
7. SWEATSHIRT
8. RUCKSACK
9. BRIEFCASE
10. FINGERLESS GLOVES

A Mighty Din

1. DINGO
2. ORDINARY
3. DINOSAUR
4. ALADDIN
5. SARDINE
6. DINGHY
7. MINDING

Written in the Clouds

1. MARY POPPINS
2. FROZEN
3. SING
4. THE NIGHTMARE BEFORE CHRISTMAS

Make It Make Make Sense – At the Zoo

1. WEBS
2. OMNIVORES
3. BAMBOO
4. ANIMALS
5. LEECHES
6. CARNIVORES
7. EAGLE
8. AMPHIBIANS
9. CONSTRICTOR
10. SQUIRRELS
11. NARWHAL

Word Ladder

BARK
BANK
SANK
SINK
WINK
LINK
LINE
FINE

Coded Capitals

1. KINGSTON, JAMAICA
2. WASHINGTON DC, USA
3. BERLIN, GERMANY
4. BEIJING, CHINA
5. MOGADISHU, SOMALIA
6. KYIV, UKRAINE
7. DHAKA, BANGLADESH

Find the Kangaroo

1. FEASTED
2. EXISTS
3. CLUE
4. ALONE
5. BURST
6. CLEANSE
7. DISMAYED
8. SLITHERED
9. UNSIGHTLY
10. INSTRUCTOR

Mixed-Up Fairy Tales
1. HANSEL AND GRETEL
2. CINDERELLA
3. SLEEPING BEAUTY
4. PUSS IN BOOTS
5. PRINCESS AND THE PEA
6. RAPUNZEL
7. SNOW WHITE
8. LITTLE RED RIDING HOOD

You've Got Nits!
1. INITIALS
2. KNITTING
3. IGNITE
4. INFINITY
5. GRANITE
6. MONITOR
7. NITROGEN
8. INCOGNITO
9. SNITCH
10. COMMUNITY

In the Supermarket
1. YOGHURT
2. CHEDDAR CHEESE
3. APPLES
4. ORANGES
5. BREAD
6. POTATOES
7. CHOCOLATE BISCUITS
8. BAKED BEANS
9. SPAGHETTI
10. TOMATOES
11. ONIONS
12. LETTUCE
13. DOUGHNUTS
14. CUCUMBER
15. FROZEN PIZZA
16. SWEETCORN
17. BUTTER
18. STRAWBERRY JAM
19. CHICKEN

What's in a Name?
1. RED
2. EARRING
3. GARDEN
4. NIAGRA
5. DIANA
6. NARNIA
7. GRAIN
8. REIGN
9. GRIND
10. DINNER
11. ENDING
12. RADAR
13. READ
14. DANGER
15. ARRANGE

Word Ladder

TALL	COOS
TAIL	COOK
BAIL	BOOK
BAWL	BOOT
BOWL	HOOT
BOWS	HOOP
COWS	

Box Words

LAMB
GOAT
DUCK
CALF

Weirdsearch – Animals Down Under

You Ran My Lord!

1. STRANGER
2. GRANDMOTHER
3. PIRANHA
4. RANK
5. CRANE
6. FRANCE
7. PRANK
8. ORANGE
9. RANDOM
10. CURRANT
11. SPORRAN
12. TRANSPORT
13. SOPRANO
14. HYDRANT
15. ENTRANCE
16. CRANBERRY
17. TARANTULA
18. RESTAURANT
19. BRANCH
20. CRANIUM

Written in the Clouds

1. PETER PAN
2. THE LION, THE WITCH AND THE WARDROBE
3. WINNIE THE POOH

Ocean Crossweird

Three is a Charm
1. READY SET GO
2. AGE BEFORE BEAUTY
3. FOUR WHEEL DRIVE
4. ANYTHING IS POSSIBLE
5. AT FIRST SIGHT
6. LESS IS MORE
7. LARGER THAN LIFE
8. MIND THE GAP

Make It Make Sense – Music
1. CLARINET/FLUTE
2. BAGUETTE/BATON
3. BELLOWS/CELLOS
4. PINCUSHION/PERCUSSION
5. SOURPUSS/SOPRANO
6. BULLDOZER/COMPOSER
7. OPERATIONS/OPERAS
8. PATCH/PIT
9. CRUMPET/TRUMPET

Scrambled Eggs
1. TOAST AND MARMALADE
2. BELGIAN WAFFLES
3. YOGHURT AND FRUIT
4. BACON AND EGGS
5. SAUSAGE ROLL
6. EGG SANDWICH
7. PORRIDGE
8. CHEESE OMELETTE
9. PANCAKES
10. ORANGE JUICE
11. FRENCH TOAST
12. MUESLI
13. COFFEE
14. TEA
15. SMOOTHIE

Fill the Refrigerator

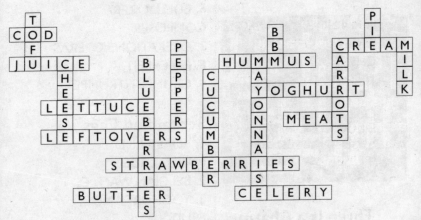

What's in a Name?

1. SPIRAL
2. WHEEL
3. WHISK
4. WHALE
5. MAPLE
6. PEA
7. WALK
8. PLEASE
9. WHISPER
10. ALASKA
11. SWILL
12. PAELLA
13. PRAM
14. WISH
15. PEARL
16. SHAWL
17. KIWI
18. SPARKLE

Cryptic Catchphrases

1. PUT YOUR BEST FOOT FORWARDS
2. HEAD IN THE CLOUDS
3. BY THE SKIN OF YOUR TEETH
4. AT THE DROP OF A HAT
5. GIVE THE COLD SHOULDER
6. HIT THE NAIL ON THE HEAD

7. COST AN ARM AND A LEG
8. PULLING YOUR LEG
9. GET IT OFF YOUR CHEST
10. PUT A FOOT IN IT

Odd one out: **AT THE DROP OF A HAT,** because the rest all mention parts of the body.

Three Little Words
1. BUNDLE OF JOY
2. SEVEN DEADLY SINS
3. BURSTING WITH PRIDE
4. CAN DO ATTITUDE
5. COME BACK SOON
6. CROSS YOUR HEART
7. DOUBLE EDGED SWORD
8. DROP DEAD GORGEOUS
9. EASY AS PIE

Riddle Words
1. ALPHABET
2. DOZENS
3. TON
4. FEW
5. ONE
6. SWIMS

Find the Joey
1. RUIN
2. STUN
3. BLOOM
4. RAGE
5. TRULY
6. SLY
7. CAVE
8. LAST
9. LIT
10. NOBLE

Hip or Hop
1. CHOP
2. HOPE
3. HOPSCOTCH
4. CHIP SHOP
5. WHOPPER
6. BISHOP
7. WHIP
8. SHIP
9. HIPPO
10. SHIPWRECK
11. HIPS

Bakers' Dozen

1. CUSTARD SLICES
2. ICED BUNS
3. SAUSAGE ROLLS
4. DANISH PASTRIES
5. JAM DOUGHNUTS
6. CHOCOLATE CHIP COOKIES
7. SCONES
8. APPLE TURNOVERS
9. BLUEBERRY MUFFINS
10. BANANA LOAVES
11. CORNISH PASTIES
12. BAKEWELL TARTS

Monumental Errors

1. COLOSSEUM
2. STATUE OF LIBERTY
3. BUCKINGHAM PALACE
4. STONEHENGE
5. TAJ MAHAL
6. EDINBURGH CASTLE
7. GIANT'S CAUSEWAY
8. GIANT PYRAMID OF GIZA

Big Top Weirdsearch

E	E	A	I	F	H	Y	A	Q	S	X	T	P	P	X
C	L	C	W	N	I	F	W	S	W	N	T	N	D	S
I	C	R	K	E	Q	R	O	C	L	O	W	N	T	L
F	Y	O	T	T	M	L	E	S	P	P	N	R	G	W
F	C	B	V	O	F	U	E	E	X	Z	O	O	J	O
O	I	A	X	Y	P	S	T	J	A	N	Z	T	U	R
X	N	T	D	R	R	H	E	S	G	T	R	N	G	N
O	U	N	F	O	C	X	A	M	O	A	E	C	G	R
B	A	Z	H	K	S	X	A	T	P	C	B	R	L	O
C	A	U	D	I	E	N	C	E	N	W	I	T	E	C
K	N	L	Y	R	E	T	S	A	M	G	N	I	R	P
D	E	P	L	A	T	E	S	P	I	N	N	E	R	O
A	G	X	C	O	N	A	I	C	I	G	A	M	Y	P
I	F	I	E	P	O	R	T	H	G	I	T	Y	D	G
E	F	V	O	L	E	N	I	L	O	P	M	A	R	T

Hink or Pinky? Have a Thinky

1. LARGE MARGE
2. NICHE QUICHE
3. BRACE CASE
4. IRON LION
5. BUSY LIZZIE
6. DAMPER CAMPER
7. MOUSE LOUSE
8. CHEESE BREEZE
9. BARN YARN
10. STENCIL PENCIL
11. COARSE SAUCE
12. ELFIE SELFIE
13. BROKEN TOKEN
14. SANDY CANDY
15. GOBBLE BOBBLE

Three is a Magic Number

1. SINK OR SWIM
2. FLIP A COIN
3. FINE AND DANDY
4. FORGIVE AND FORGET
5. GAME SET MATCH
6. GET CARRIED AWAY
7. GOING FOR BROKE
8. HANDLE WITH CARE
9. HEART OF GOLD

What's in a Name?

1. MILES
2. LIONESS
3. LIMO
4. MOBILE
5. LEMON
6. MINE
7. SNOB
8. NEMESIS
9. MISSION
10. MINOS
11. SIMON
12. NESSIE
13. MISSILE
14. SON
15. MILNE
16. SOLEMN

Gordon Have Morsey!

Translation: Mr Palmer from next door let his dog Gordon in your garden. Gordon is digging. Take a picture. Show your mum.

1. GORDON THE DOG
2. MR PALMER
3. NEXT DOOR
4. NEELAY WILL SHOW A PICTURE TO HIS MUM.

Word Ladder

KING
KIND
MIND
MINE
MANE
LANE
LAME
TAME
TIME
MIME
MICE

Missing Type

1. BULLDOG, POODLE, LABRADOR, BLOODHOUND
TYPE: DOG

2. PYTHON, COBRA, CONSTRICTOR, RATTLE
TYPE: SNAKE

3. MONK, HADDOCK, COD, SALMON
TYPE: FISH

Cat with Nine Lives

1. CATTLE
2. SCATTY
3. DELICATE
4. INTRICATE
5. CATER
6. LOCATION
7. CATSUIT
8. CATHEDRAL

What's in a Name?

1. RETURN
2. HEART
3. TARGET
4. TRUTH

5. TUG
6. HUG
7. GARNET
8. TEEN
9. NUGGET
10. URGENT
11. ARTHUR
12. GUT
13. AGENT
14. BURGER
15. BUTTER

School Bag Weirdsearch

V	G	L	Y	V	S	C	I	S	S	O	R	S	T	K
H	M	L	L	U	N	C	H	B	O	X	O	D	E	P
O	P	P	U	K	F	O	L	D	E	R	R	R	X	E
M	V	R	H	E	C	E	X	L	Z	P	X	I	T	N
E	H	W	O	I	S	R	O	T	X	E	Z	N	B	C
W	N	S	C	T	G	T	A	A	H	N	G	K	O	I
O	O	S	T	A	R	H	I	Y	S	S	V	S	O	L
R	T	H	R	I	L	A	L	C	O	E	O	B	K	C
K	E	A	P	R	C	C	C	I	K	N	R	O	W	A
R	B	R	E	U	P	K	U	T	G	B	S	T	H	S
Y	O	P	N	L	E	R	Y	L	O	H	J	T	O	E
C	O	E	C	E	K	I	Q	T	A	R	T	L	I	C
U	K	N	I	R	I	U	V	T	A	T	D	E	O	S
S	H	E	L	D	T	F	L	C	A	P	O	W	R	N
D	M	R	S	R	U	B	B	E	R	W	E	R	N	V

Box Words
MONKEY
JAGUAR
BEAVER
COUGAR
DONKEY
GIBBON

But In
1. BELLYBUTTON
2. BUTCHER
3. BUTTERNUT
4. HALIBUT
5. BUTE
6. BUTLER
7 BUTTERCUP
8. BUTTY
9. BUTTOCKS
10. BUTTRESS
11. BUTTERFLY
12. DEBUT
13. CONTRIBUTE
14. BUTTER FINGERS

Mixed-Up Subjects
1. GEOGRAPHY
2. HISTORY
3. MATHS
4. ENGLISH
5. SCIENCE
6. FRENCH
7. SPANISH
8. ART AND DESIGN
9. MUSIC
10. COMPUTING

What's in a Name?
1. GOLF
2. FIGHT
3. CLOTHE
4. FOREIGN
5. ALTON
6. RHINO
7. TRIFLE
8. THRONE
9. FETCH
10. NITROGEN
11. ANNIE
12. CONIFER
13. CRINGE
14. ARCHIE
15. LOCH

273

Missing Type

1. RUBY, SAPPHIRE, PEARL, EMERALD
TYPE: JEWEL

2. WRAPPING, WRITING, TISSUE, DRAWING
TYPE: PAPER

3. STEEL, ALUMINIUM, PLATINUM, LEAD, SILVER
TYPE: METAL

Box Words

CAMEL
KOALA
EAGLE
TIGER
ZEBRA

Cryptogram Concertos

1. BLOW YOUR OWN TRUMPET
2. PLAYING SECOND FIDDLE
3. MARCH TO THE BEAT OF YOUR OWN DRUM
4. BREAK A LEG
5. PREACH TO THE CHOIR
6. ALL BELLS AND WHISTLES
7. FACE THE MUSIC
8. PUMP UP THE JAM
9. IT TAKES TWO TO TANGO
10. CHANGE YOUR TUNE
11. DANCE LIKE NOBODY IS WATCHING

Odd one out: number four as the rest are musical.

Car Box Words

4 LETTERS
HORN
AXLE
BOOT
TYRE

5 LETTERS
RADIO
WHEEL
BRAKE
GEARS
LIGHT

Body Parts

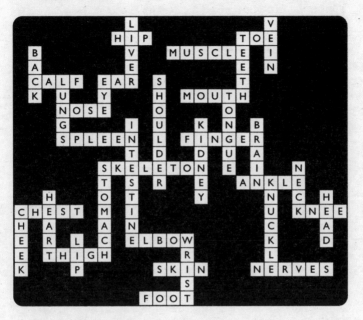

Bonus Hinkety Pinketies

1. PERCUSSION DISCUSSION
2. PRESIDENT'S RESIDENCE
3. POTTERY LOTTERY
4. CANTALOUPE ANTELOPE
5. HISTORY MYSTERY
6. SODIUM PODIUM
7. MARTIME PANTOMIME
8. FAKERY BAKERY

NOTES